FUNDAMENTALS OF THE SOVIET SYSTEM

The Soviet Weightlifting System
and modern applications to the sport of weightlifting

Gwendolyn Sisto and Ivan Rojas

Printed in the United States of America
by Lightning Source, Inc.

ISBN 978-1-943650-40-8

Photo credits: Ivan Rojas, Gwendolyn Sisto and Hookgrip

Published by BookCrafters, Parker, Colorado
Joe and Jan McDaniel SAN-859-6352
http://bookcrafters.net

Copies of this book may be ordered from:
http://ristosports.com /conferences/training/books/

About the Authors

Gwendolyn Sisto is one of the top 69kg weightlifters in the USA and has competed for Team USA on at least four occasions. She competed at the 2008 Olympic Trials. Gwen is also a Rocket Scientist. She holds a Masters of Science in Aeronautics and Astronautics from MIT and a Bachelors of Science in Aerospace Engineering from Georgia Tech. She has worked in the high-tech aerospace industry for over 10 years.

She enjoys applying her scientific background to studying and improving training methods and technique.

Ivan Rojas is a renowned coach and former international weightlifter. He has coached numerous National Teams in the sport of weightlifting.

His record includes:
• Coach of the 2015 Panama Pan Am Games Team
• Coach of the 2010 USA World University Team, which won 15 medals (most successful team in last 30 years)
• Coach of the 2014 13 and under USA Youth Women's Team
• Coach of the 2015 Panama World Team

He has studied weightlifting behind the Iron Curtain in the former Soviet Union, as well as Bulgaria, Cuba, and East Germany. He was the first American to ever be permitted into the Chinese National team training hall and study the training of their National team (most successful at the 2008 Olympics). He has studied in Kazakhstan, the most successful weightlifting team of the 2012 Olympics, and even lectured on training methodologies to Kazakhstan National Coaches.

Gwen and *Ivan* have combined their love for weightlifting and engineering by founding Risto Sports. Together, they have brought the best weightlifting training, shoes, singlets, and wrist wraps to the world.

http://www.ristosports.com

Other publications:
 Ivan Rojas (2015) *Kazakhstan Weightlifting System for Elite Athletes*
 Gwendolyn Sisto (2010) *Assessing Stakeholder Salience Through the View of Lean Enterprise Transformation*

Contents

Who should read this book

Anyone who wants to improve their or their athlete totals in weightlifting.

The methods presented in the book are based on fact; the Soviet system methods have proven results. These sample programs are not based on internet rumors or opinion, they're based on the training and recovery of Russian athletes who repeatedly won olympic medals. This book can teach anyone with a basic knowledge of weightlifting how to program their training and how to recover. In effect, anyone with a basic understanding of the olympic lifts and safe weightlifting techniques can use this book to improve their weightlifting totals.

This book is written such that all levels of weightlifters and coaches can get something out of it. And, the book covers standard programming terminology, explaining it in detail; this will help people new to the sport. It will also help coaches communicate with other coaches in the same universally accepted technical terms. This book also covers advanced topics which even very experienced coaches will find interesting and be able use to grow their knowledge.

Gwendolyn Sisto and Ivan Rojas

Testimonials

"Ivan and Gwen at Risto sports are pioneers at educating their methods in modern Olympic lifting. Many programs and books don't help the athlete understand programming, how to build out a program, and also how to raise or lower it for different implementations. This book is a great sample of the "whys" behind a program— not just merely facts spit onto paper. Ivan and Gwen have worked with top athletes from around the world but also work with many local level athletes allowing them to make the beginner feel like they are being treated like the pro's."

Matt Adamcheck, Head Coach & owner of 4 Star Strength

"A powerful book for any strength coach to have in their arsenal. Like it or loathe it, the basis for ALL periodization programs stem from the original work the Soviets did. This book gives a solid review of that system with privilege to source material that few others could even hope to have, enabling it to provide a perspective second only to actually having visited and trained there yourself. In studying this material you stand to gain insight on how the largely successful Soviet coaches viewed the minutia details of a program and how they played on their athletes. Having been a student of one of Russia's greatest coaches, Boris Sheiko, I can tell you from first hand experience that these methods are anything but dated and useless. Quite the opposite; in fact the methods covered here can be used to create devastatingly effective programs, and in the hands of a master provide a coach the tools to orchestrate a concert of volume and intensity culminating in a championship performance. The Soviet method does not try to sell you with sexy buzz words. Instead it is based on solid empirical science whose only missing component is brutally hard work in order to bring it to life. As mentioned in the book, once you come to grasp the concepts outlined you can apply them to virtually any other sport or program you wish to see results in. I cannot recommend reading this book enough, and then to continue your studies further into the origins and history of the Soviet era programming science."

Jance Footit, 5 Rings Barbell

"*Fundamentals of the Soviet System* by Risto Sports is a modern review of the programming used by, arguably, the most successful machine ever devised to produce world-class weightlifters with long careers. Content ranges from theory to detailed day-to-day implementation, with over 50 pages of set-by-set, 12 week macrocycles for athletes training 3,4, 5 and 6 days a week—recreational to elite level athletes. The authors ride a great line between the two objectives of giving big picture reasons for the classic Soviet approach and providing a manual for coaches faced with the everyday realities of training weightlifters in the United States. "

Scott Glasgow, USAW National Coach, President and Head Coach of Utah Barbell

Gwendolyn Sisto and Ivan Rojas

Acknowledgements and Foreword

The initial material and framework for this book was created for and given to the authors by **Dr. Alfredo Herrera** who was, at the time, the Technical Director of Risto Sports. His material was based on his years of first hand work in the Soviet Union and other major weightlifting powers like Cuba and Colombia. The original portions from the doctor were about 20 PowerPoint slides of text and figures in Russian and Spanish. Many of the figures are his own or from his mentor **Arkady Medvedev**, with whom he worked, and who gave him a personal copy of the material.

We have since translated it, expounded on the Doctor's materials, edited it significantly to improve its comprehension, and added significant portions of material based on our combined 50+ years of experience studying this system. Additionally, we wrote the book such that beginner and advanced audiences can understand it; the original work assumed a high level of comprehension. For example, you will see technical terms defined and explained so even those newest to the sport can learn the most important jargon. We have also added commentary to make this material more applicable for the part of our audience in the Western world, where most weightlifting is not state-sponsored and is privatized. Unaltered material from the doctor is cited as such. We also strive to cite Soviet authors such as Medvedev where possible, and where information is beyond generalities.

We would like to acknowledge 1980 Olympic Champion and owner of 20 World Records, **Daniel Nunez**. Daniel has been the mentor of Ivan Rojas for many years and has trained extensively in the Soviet System. He has contributed additional insights and clarity into the system.

We would also like to thank **Scott Glasgow**, a professor of mathematics at Brigham Young University, for taking the time to critique the book, particularly its readability. There were quite a few Russian-isms and areas that needed further explanation and, who better than an esteemed college professor with numerous published works to point them out?

Gwendolyn Sisto and Ivan Rojas

What is the Soviet System?

The Soviet System is a holistic approach to training for the olympic sport of weightlifting. It includes a scientific approach to designing training programs, a philosophical basis, and recovery systems.

It was developed in the Soviet Union or USSR in the 20th century by Soviet researchers, as well as researchers from other communist countries, particularly, Cuba. In effect, many of the researchers cited in this book were from what is now modern day Russia and Cuba.

It produced hundreds of olympic medals, World championship medals, and, of course, world records. It is still in use, today, continuing to generate weightlifting glory.

The Soviet system is the basis for all modern weightlifting systems. Many coaches in modern Russia, China, North Korea, and Cuba use the Soviet System. Other highly successful countries like Bulgaria, Kazakhstan, Greece (Nat Arem, 2016), and Colombia are either derivative of the Soviet system or use the soviet system for developing athletes prior to the olympic level (Ivan Rojas, 2015).

Photo 1 - Lioa Hui of China clean and jerking 193kg at 77kg at the 2014 World Championships. China's weightlifting system is derivative of the Soviet System and was heavily influenced by Soviet Researcher Alexey Medvedev's work there. Photo by Ivan Rojas

Founders of the Soviet System

The specialists that founded the modern Russian System; including, the Scientific grounds, methodology and practical application of the system.

The two main founders of the Soviet System were **Arkady Nikitich Vorobiev** (1924- 2012) and **Alexey Medvedev Sidorovich** (1927-2003). Both were lifters in the Soviet Union; later turned coaches and programming theorists. Although they may have started from similar training backgrounds, their approach to the programming and training for the sport became nuancedly different.

Vorobiev:

Arkady Vorobiev won two Olympic gold medals in 1956 and 1960 in weightlifting. He was a four time World champion in the years 1954, 1955, 1957, and 1958. He also won silver at the World Championships in 1959 and bronze medal in 1961. Vorobiev was also a three time European champion in the years 1954, 1955, and 1958, and he also took the silver in 1959 and bronze in 1961. He set 21 middle-heavyweight world records – nine in snatch, three in clean and jerk, two in press, and seven in the total (Hererra, 2012).

In addition to being a weightlifter, Vorobiev was a remarkable scientist. Even more impressive, he commenced his scientific achievements while he was still a competitive athlete for the Soviet Union. During his sports career, he graduated from the Medical Institute and defended a dissertation for the Candidate of Science degree in 1962. In 1970, he defended a dissertation for the Doctor of Medical Science degree at the Institute of Aviation and Space Medicine in Moscow. In 1977, Vorobiev was the Rector of the Moscow Oblast Institute of Physical Culture and Sports. In 1995, he was elected to the International Weightlifting Federation Hall of Fame (Hererra, 2012).

Vorobiev's research areas included application of weightlifting training to cosmonauts (astronauts from the USSR). Russian cosmonauts would lose too much muscle in space, hence Vorobiev studied protocols to reduce muscle atrophy in space.

Medvedev:

Alexey Medvedev Sidorovich (1927-2003) was also a decorated competitive weightlifter and coach. In 1957 and 1958, Medvedev won the world title in the heavyweight category. Alexander Medvedev was also the first Soviet Weightlifter and third in the world to reach a total of 500 kg (Hererra, 2012). Note, during his weightlifting career, prior to 1976, there were 3 lifts– snatch, clean and jerk, and the clean and press.

In 1962, Medvedev became the coach of the national weightlifting team of the USSR (Hererra, 2012). In 1964, he prepared 3 Olympic champions for the USSR (A. Vahonina, R. Plufelderand , I. Jabotinsky). Alexander Medvedev worked as head of weightlifting at the Russian State University of physical culture, sport and tourism. Under his leadership, the Department has done a lot to prepare weightlifting specialists not only for Russia but from other countries: Cuba, China, Poland, Bulgaria, DPRK.

Likewise, he was invited to many countries. He traveled to China many times, lecturing at Beijing University of Physical Culture (Hererra, 2012). He provided practical assistance to China's weightlifting team, and, consequently, he received the title of Honorary Professor of Beijing University of Physical Culture. He was the first weightlifter to receive this honorary degree.

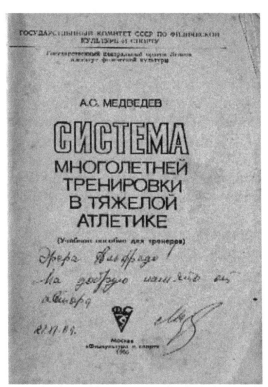

Figure 2 - Photo of the cover page of Medvedev's seminal book with a signed message to Dr. Alfredo Herrera (Herrera, 2012)

Photo 2 - Ri Jong Hwa of North Korea clean and jerking 133kg. PRK's system was highly influenced by Medvedev.
Photo by Ivan Rojas

The Architecture of the Soviet System

Table 1 (page 12) describes the key components which come together to make the Soviet System. The goal of the Soviet System is to increase competitive results, or , in other words, increase a weightlifter's total at competitions.

The elements of the system include the leveraging the principles of various scientific disciplines such as mechanics, mathematics, biology, and biochemistry. These are referred to as "concepts". The "objects" are the actual things the weightlifter and coach are doing to increase performance – training program, recuperation systems, and nutrition. Whereas, a successful training program requires to be managed to the individual lifter, and its success is predicated on a good diet and good, intentioned, rest by the athlete. The "subjects" are the people applying the "concepts" and carrying out the "objects".

Main Goal	Increase Competitive Results	
Elements of the system	Concepts	Principles of mechanics, mathematics, biology, biochemistry and others
	Objects	Management of training loading, recuperative systems, Nutrition and others
	Subjects	Lifters, coaches, medical staff and others
Interaction of groups of elements with similar properties	- Level of development of GPP, Technique, psychology, and theory - Period of biological and psychological adaptation - Mathematical models for diagnosis and forecast	
Theoretical fundamentals	- General Theory of sports training - Teaching systems - Biomechanics, Physiology and chemistry of physical activity	
Philosophy	- Materialism of natural science - Hegel's idealistic dialectic system - Realism	

Table 1 - Science, methodology, and philosophy behind the modern weightlifting system. Source Dr Herrera

Philosophy of the Soviet System

Hegel's dialectic

To understand the Soviet system, its philosophies must be understood first. The Soviet System uses the basic principles of Hegel's dialectic – thesis, antithesis, and synthesis. A theorist would come up with a thesis or a new idea. Another theorist would have an opposing idea or antithesis. The goal would be to create a synthesis of the two opposing ideas to get a new more effective idea- the synthesis. Later on, this new synthesis, after more research and investigation, would become a new thesis. And, hence, the cycle of knowledge production could start again.

In other words, the Soviets cared about what worked, and what could be proven to work. This is further explained by their embracing realism, pragmatism, materialism of natural science.

Pragmatism

Soviet system was essentially pragmatic. If a theory worked, it was accepted and applied. If something works, then it is good. Researchers and coaches had freedom to try different approaches as long as they got results. As long as the science did not criticize the ideology of the central government (historic materialism), then the research was permitted. This fit into Hegel's dialectic as researchers and coaches were always looking to select the best idea that worked or synthesize ideas to get a superior result (Rosenthal, 1964).

Realism

The real world is whatever exists outside of subjectivity, outside of your mind (Rosenthal, 1964). This is independent of what believe the real world is.

Materialism of Natural science

Scientists interpret nature based on practical data and experimentation (Rosenthal, 1964). For something to exist, it must be able to be empirically proven. All facts can be scientifically proven.

In summary, the material presented in the following pages is the result of rigorous scientific research. Anything presented as a fact was at some point proven to exist via an experiment. The programming and recovery systems presented in the following sections were used on real athletes to produce real results, such as Olympic Gold medals.

Element	Relationship with competitive results weightlifting
Static Maximum Strength	Not a direct relationship. This is not an indicator of genetic potential for weightlifting. Not all strong athletes are to be great weightlifters.
Relative Strength	Direct relationship. Athletes who lift more for their bodyweight than competitors in the same or higher weight class, in general, will be more successful. This is related to determining the ideal weight class for an athlete predicated on height and body size.
Strength relation between flexor and extensor muscles	Direct relationship. This is salient to maintaining an optimal strength ratio between flexor and extensor. This is important for preventing injury and optimizing power output.
Increase of muscle mass	Direct relationship. Increase of muscle mass will enable increased performance ability.
Muscle power	Direct relationship. Muscle power is defined as work applied over time. It can forecast sports performance.
Quality and frequency of nerve impulses to muscles	Direct relationship. This is relevant to finding the optimal number of repetitions by intensity zone and the quality of muscle contractions.
Function of the Central Nervous System	Direct relationship. Hormonal changes governed by the CNS affects performance, especially related to medium to large training loads.

Table 2 - Elements commonly associated with weightlifting and their relationship to competitive sports performance in weightlifting (Hererra, 2012)

Strategies and methods for increasing competitive sports performance

The term "sports performance" is used, generally, to describe the athlete's ability to "perform" or succeed during competition in their respective sport. The strategies and methods presented in this following chapter are aimed at increasing the "competitive results" or the weightlifter's total at a competition. These methods were developed on research, for the most part, on Soviet adult male weightlifters[1] (Hererra, 2012). They have been applied successfully to female[2] weightlifters. Interestingly, many of the strategies presented in this chapter can be beneficial for strength athletes in general.

To increase Competitive Sports Results, the athlete must increase their muscle strength and their body's ability to produce said strength. Hence, it is important to understand what types of muscle strength are discussed in sport and which types are directly related to improving a weightlifter's total.

Table 2 (page 14) introduces different elements commonly thought of when coaches seek to increase an athlete's weightlifting total. The elements with a "direct relationship" are most important to weightlifters and are discussed further in this chapter.

Static Maximum Strength

Static Maximum strength is the maximum force a muscle group can apply. It is important in sports that have isometric contracts, where the athlete is holding a position for some amount of time. In weightlifting, the movements are dynamic, and the olympic lifts are executed in seconds. In effect, static strength, by itself, is an unreliable indicator of genetic potential in weightlifters. For example, many strong athlete's fail to become successful weightlifters because they are not explosive enough.

 It is true, that, as the weightlifter's career progresses, their static strength will increase. However, increase in static strength is not proportional with increases in the Snatch and the Clean and Jerk (Hererra, 2012). For example, weightlifters can apply the equivalent of lifting 500kg (of Static Maximum Strength) or more in the beginning of the second phase of the pull (Hererra, 2012), and this is far more than any snatch or clean and jerk lifted in competition. That being said, it may be possible to be use static maximum strength as a secondary indicator of genetic potential, if it were correlated to the excitability of the central nervous system during training (Hererra, 2012).

---

1   Interestingly, many of the strategies presented in this chapter can be beneficial for just about any type of strength athlete.
2   One of Dr. Herrera's most famous female athletes was Olympic Gold Medalist Maria Isabel Urrutia from Colombia. He had applied this system prior to her winning a World Championship.

In regard to training program design for a competitive weightlifter, static strength is an output, an externality or a side benefit of training. It is not the sole goal of training, nor the core focus of the training program. Thus, static strength training systems[3] are not important for weightlifters.

Relative Strength

Relative strength is a measure of how much an athlete lifts in comparison to their size. In America, we compare athletes of different bodyweights by using the cliché "pound for pound strongest" lifter.

Relative strength has a direct relation with increase of sports quality (Hererra, 2012). The expected height for each bodyweight class was established methodically by the Soviets. In effect, body weight and weight loss control systems were also established to keep athletes within a certain height range in weight classes statistically suited for their height.

Figure 3 shows empirically established height range for each weight class.

Рост (см) у атлетов различной квалификации (по материалам изучения более 500 спортсменов)				
Весовая категория, кг	Квалификация			
	III р.	II р.	I р.	мс
52	160,8±1,3	156,5±1,4	153,9±1,1	153,7±1,2
56	161,5±1,4	159,5±1,4	157,1±0,9	154,7±0,9
60	166,5±1,2	163,1±1,1	160,1±0,9	156,9±0,8
67,5	169,0±1,0	167,6±1,1	166,6±1,0	161,6±0,8
75	173,5±1,0	171,8±0,9	169,7±0,9	167,4±0,8
82,5	175,0±1,9	175,5±1,1	174,9±0,7	171,2±0,7
90	177,7±0,6	179,4±1,0	177,8±0,8	175,7±1,2
100	180,9±0,9	180,4±0,4	177,4±1,2	176,2±1,3
110	181,7±0,7	180,8±0,3	180,2±0,9	177,5±1,2
Свыше 110	184,4±0,5	182,2±0,1	181,5±0,6	183,9±1,3

Figure 3 - Ideal height for each weight class by skill level (Medvedev, 1985)

The left column shows the bodyweight of the athlete. The 4 columns on the right show the average height and standard deviation (the +/- value which describes the spread of data on either side of the average or "mean") for each weight class. The columns increase by skill level. Note, the bodyweights shown follow the former men's weight classes during the height of the Soviet weightlifting era and were the official weight classes until the late 1980's. The table illustrates that

---

3   For example, static training systems for powerlifting are not important for weightlifters.

athletes of a higher skill level will typically have a smaller height for the same body mass. This is expected as the athlete will put on more lean muscle mass and increase their bone density as they train from a beginner to an Olympic level athlete.

Figure 4 shows the updated chart with the current men's weight classes:

DIV	56	62	69	77	85	94	105	105 plus
HEIGHT	4'9"	5'2"	5'4"	5'5"	5'6"	5'7"	5'8"	6'
DIFF +/-	1.18 Inch	1.18 Inch	1.18 Inch	1.18 Inch	1.18 Inch	1.18 Inch	1.18 Inch	1.96 Inch

Figure 4 - Optimal height range for each weight class (Europe, 2011-2016)

The height values in **Figure 4** are the mean or average. The "DIFF" column shows the standard deviation, which means there will always be athletes that fall outside the average plus or minus the standard deviation—just that it is more likely the athlete's body mass and heights will fit with in these means plus or minus the standard deviation. Thus, this chart can be used as a guide to plan an athlete's mass gain with skill level. Of course, there will always be outlier athletes that may not fit the standard deviation. The charts are meant to describe the majority of the population.

In terms of applicability to female lifters, we can speculate that slightly higher heights in relation to bodyweight will occur due to anthropological differences between the skeletal structure of men versus women. For example, men tend to have larger hearts, lungs, and bones. A new chart for women has not yet been created. As of the Houston 2015 World Championships, research was still being done on it.

Relation of strength between the flexor and extensor muscles

With the increase of quality training, the ratio of strength between the flexor and extensor muscles is enhanced.

Empirical studies show the following desirable ratios of flexor to extensor muscle groups for weightlifters (Hererra, 2012):

Muscle group	Strength ratio (flexor:extensor)
Muscles of the arm	1.6:1
Trunk	4.3:1
Leg	5.4:1
Thighs	4.3:1

Table 3 - Strength ratios of Flexor and Extensor muscles

Strength applied on time, muscle power

Power has a close relationship with competitive results, particularly, to evaluate and forecast competition performance. It is evaluated by jumping. It can be tested by either long jump or vertical jump. For example, Olympic Champion Yuri Vardanian's highest competition result correlated with his static high jump of 3 feet 4 inches and a long jump of 11 feet (Hererra, 2012).

Frequency and quality of nerve impulses

For the increase of competition performance--not only is the quantity of muscle mass important-- the optimal frequency of nerve impulses and the capacity of recruiting motor units quickly are also important (Hererra, 2012). This varies depending on the fatigue of the muscle, such as frequency when contractions are performed at 70% of maximum strength with 3-4 reps. Methodically, the frequency of nerve impulses and capacity to quickly recruit motor units are of great importance for training intensity zones, starting at intensities of 60%, 60-69%; 70-79%;80-89%;90-100% of personal record. Likewise, the frequency of nerve impulses and recruiting of motor units in athletes were used to define the optimal number of repetitions per intensity zone, and these are especially crucial in the 90-100% of maximum intensity zone. The sample programs in the back of this book employ optimal repetition ranges with consideration of the above.

Excitability of the central nervous system

The ability to place the Central Nervous System in an excited state, was shown to increase strength over baseline by 10%, which translates to increased competition results. The increase of muscle strength results from the segregation of hormones of quick action,[4] such as adrenaline and noradrenaline, as well as the neurotransmitter acetylcholine[5] (Hererra, 2012). Experimentation showed that training with medium to high loading caused the quantity of noradrenaline in the blood to double, the quantity of HGH to increase, and increase in blood cortisone levels (Hererra, 2012)Hormones segregated by the supra-adrenal glands also increased their presence in the athlete's blood, among them corticoids (Herrera, 2012).

Hormonal changes

Hormonal changes have direct influence in catabolism or recovery. Optimally leveraging hormonal changes leads to increasing the training loading and as a collateral result the increase of muscle mass (Hererra, 2012). In other words, the athlete's natural hormonal cycle will affect performance.

Synthetic hormones have been used, but their secondary effects are harmful for the athlete and, ethically, aren't acceptable. For these reasons, these substances are banned and penalized (doping, COI, WADA) (Hererra, 2012).

Nevertheless, researchers also look for permissible ways to optimize hormones naturally through

---

4   "quick action" hormones are secreted in the adrenal glands.
5   Acetylcholine is a neurotransmitter that works to activate muscles.

the usage of natural and legal products. Many permissible supplements can affect hormones. For example, growth hormone levels are affected by amino-acids, particularly, lysine, ornithine, and arginine. Carnitine has also been used widely.

Endogenously produced, steroid hormones such as Vitamin D,[6] estrogen, pregnenolone, and testosterone are affected by other mechanisms. It is up to the athlete to have comprehensive bloodwork done to determine which natural supplements may aid in optimizing their natural hormone levels. One supplement plan will not work for every athlete; it must be individualized.

Means and Methodology to optimize the Training loading

- Daily Training regime
- Effect of time of day on motor capabilities
- Recovery
     Sleep
     Nutrition
- Training in conditions of moderated Hypoxia
- Influence of cold -an integral view

Figure 5 - Photo of *Anatoly Karapaty* (USSR) covers the wall of the Astana Training Center in Kazakhstan, serving as a reminder that many great weightlifting countries have roots in the Soviet System. Photo by Gwendolyn Rojas.

---

6   Vitamin D is actually a steroid hormone, although the general public views it as a "vitamin."

Daily Training Regime

Adaptation of the athlete is a cumulative process, where training loads are combined with rest periods. This is one of the Russian principles of daily training: "relation between training and rest" (Hererra, 2012). This is the reason for which daily training and rest are the foundation of competitive performance.

Effect of time of day on motor capabilities

Motor capabilities during the day have peaks and troughs, depending on climate, phylogenetic factors and lifestyle. Early in the morning after getting up, 6AM for example, the motor capabilities are proper for aerobic activity; around 10 am, for speed and strength; after lunch, the capabilities go down. In the early afternoon hours, capabilities are good for flexibility work (Hererra, 2012). In the late afternoon, motor capabilities are better for strength and, especially, explosive strength.

Methodically, in the morning, it is advised to work light aerobic exercises; then, later, work resistance force such as squats and pulls. In the afternoon, it is advised to work explosive lifts such as snatch and C&J. If the lifter has a third session, isolated exercises are advised, specifically antagonistic muscles.

Recovery

Sleep
Sleep is a fundamental time in which recovery of muscle tissue occurs. It's advised to sleep 7-8 hours a day and 30 minutes after lunch (Hererra, 2012).

Nutrition
Caloric expenditure during training of the lifter can vary between 200 and 800 kilocalories (Hererra, 2012). The energetic burn isn't high and exhaustion in calories isn't high either. In other words, weightlifting does not burn a lot of calories in comparison to other Olympic Sports.

However, the exhaustion of phosphates is high (Hererra, 2012). Control of phosphate expenditure can be met with diet and supplement modifications.

Protein is the most important macro-nutrient for competitive weightlifters. It's advised 1 gram of protein per kilogram of body weight. Nutrition of the lifter leans towards protein from milk and its products, meat, fish, and natural gelatin which contains glutamine (Hererra, 2012). Glutamine is the amino acid with a significant presence in the muscle and plays an essential role in the recovery of the tissue. Carbs and fats should be controlled to avoid the increase of body fat composition.

In terms of understanding which amino acids a lifter may need to take, it is advised that the lifter have bloodwork done. An Amino acid panel, which is ordered by a licensed medical professional in most places, will tell the lifter which amino acids their diet and supplementation is efficiently supplementing, including glutamine. Again, amino acids are key for natural growth hormone production and growth of muscles. Not all amino acids are equally important for sports performance and optimal natural hormone levels.

Training in conditions of moderated Hypoxia

Training at high altitudes for short periods of time can assist in improving Athletic performance. A training period of 3 weeks in moderate altitude (7874 feet over sea level)has shown influence in increase of maximum strength between 10% and 30% (Hererra, 2012). Elite athletes train at this altitude for 21 day periods (Hererra, 2012). In other words, it is not necessary to train at high altitude all year long. High altitude training is ideal for focused training camps in the preparatory phases of training.

Influence of cold – An integral View

Recent research has contradicted the long held belief that the icing of muscles improves recovery (Jam, 2014). Such studies cite that inflammation can be good for muscle repair, hence icing to reduce inflammation is undesirable. That being said, it is not uncommon for scientists focusing on one specific subject or field to be completely unaware of other fields of research and how a mechanism they are studying impacts other fields. The following sections take an integral look at icing or chryotherapy, describing how it is used in the Soviet System and the biological mechanisms that it likely affects to improve training.

The primary goal of icing is to create beneficial, natural hormonal changes
Cold has been shown to stimulate some receptors with positive effects. Theoretically, it's known that thermic stimulation speeds the recovery process, because it increases local blood circulation and also stimulates the hormonal system (Hererra, 2012). Experimentation has shown that cold showers between weightlifting exercises has increased the work capability for the next exercise (Hererra, 2012). In practice, it is recommended at the end of workout application of cold to the areas affected by training to prevent injuries. In high level training, it's advised thermic contrast alternating cold and hot (Hererra, 2012). In Russian training centers, athletes finish training with sauna and cold water pools (Herrera, 2012). Often, athletes use them at the end of the training week (Rojas, 2014). Icing the kidney area for 15 minutes after training has also shown positive results (Hererra, 2012); this is not surprising as adrenal glands are located by the kidneys. Cubans have also rubbed ice on their legs, shoulders, and low back between exercises (Rojas, 2014). Anecdotally, Cuban Olympic Gold Medalist, Daniel Nunez credits his 20 World Records and Olympic Gold medal to ice therapy (Nunez, 2014).

Inductive reasoning: Hormonal mechanisms for increased performance due to cold
In terms of the hormonal effects of cold, cold clearly impacts the adrenal system, which in turn impacts the athlete's ability to train. For example, studies have shown that animals with removed adrenal glands are incapable of tolerating the cold. Likewise, the adrenal functions of humans have enabled us to survive and settle cold regions throughout the earth (Paakkonen & Leppaluoto, 2002). In effect, exposure to cold can increase adrenal hormones.

Short term cold exposure can increase cortisol and norepinephrine (Paakkonen & Leppaluoto, 2002), both essential for athletes. One study found that even exposure to cold air for just 5 minutes at 4º C raised plasma norepinephrine (Paakkonen & Leppaluoto, 2002). Norepinephrine is a stress hormone triggered by the sympathetic nervous systems. It triggers the fight or flight response. In weightlifting we use the sympathetic nervous system to execute maximal lifts in a reflex like reaction. Norepinephrine causes increased heart rate and enables muscles to work faster and more efficiently. Further, it is desirable to lift with an elevated heart rate, to keep the muscles warm and ready to output power. This hormone also increases glucose, which is an energy source for a weightlifter's muscles. Therefore, increasing norepinephrine via the influence of cold may be one mechanism to explain the positive impact of cold therapy used extensively by the Cubans and the Soviets.

It is important also to address the role of cortisol. Cortisol is needed to deal with the stress of training and inflammation. It is ideal that cortisol levels should follow a circadian rhythm and training times are optimally arranged around the athlete's circadian rhythm, whereas too low cortisol levels and too high cortisol levels are both negatives.

Further buttressing Soviet claims, scientists have also proven that cold exposure can allow an athlete to exert direct control over the sympathetic nervous system (Anne Houtman, 2016). In the case of Wim Hof, "the iceman", who regularly completes athletic feats in below freezing environments, scientists found that he was able to influence his immune response and the hormones epinephrine, norepinephrine, and cortisol with cold exposure (Anne Houtman, 2016). Hof's technique for hormonal manipulation involved cold exposure combined with breathing exercises and meditation (Anne Houtman, 2016). Scientists found that with ice exposure for 30 minutes, Hof increased his cortisol levels and decreased inflammation. Hof also displayed higher brown fat levels, which contain more mitochondria than white fat (Hof, 2015). This assists in rapid energy production, in Hof's case , to produce body heat (Hof, 2015). The implications on athletes is interesting, in terms of rapid energy production.

Though Hof had stellar results with prolonged cold exposure, it is important to note that the cold exposure used by Soviets and their Cuban allies were done under short durations. Other studies have shown that long term exposure to cold can decrease thyroid hormones T3 free and T4 free (Paakkonen & Leppaluoto, 2002) . It is unclear if this can be generalized to the Hof case as well.

In summary, Cold exposure can increase norepinephrine and epinephrine, which could ready the body for the next exercise. Cold exposure can also increase cortisol to deal with inflammation, also enabling the body to continue with exercise at a high performance level.

Direct experience with ice therapy at Risto Sports
In the training of Rocio Navarro, a member of the Panamanian National Team in the 69kg weight category, ice therapy along with Soviet System programming enabled her to advance from a national level lifter to an elite level lifter in Pan America.

Figure 6 - *Rocio Navarro* clean and jerking 113kg at the 2015 Pan Am Games, photo by Ivan Rojas

Once at Risto Sports, Coach Ivan significantly increased Rocio's volume and introduced her to ice therapy. She would ice her legs religiously after every work out. She had never done cryotherapy prior to coming to Risto Sports.

In a 6 month time period, Rocio achieved huge improvements. She went from a 145kg back squat, 83kg snatch, and 107kg clean and jerk to a 175kg back squat, 92kg snatch, and a 115kg clean and jerk with training lifts of 96kg and 119kg, respectively. This is a 13% improvement, whereas, mature athletes at the international level are seeking to improve, realistically, 4.8% a year.

In competition, Rocio was able to out lift Cuban and Venezuelan lifters. Both of these countries have a long storied tradition of elite weightlifting and are always expected to pummel any lifters from Panama. The Cuban coach later conferred to Coach Ivan Rojas, Panama's National Coach and of Risto Sports, that he was in utter shock to see such improvement in the Panamanian lifter.

In conclusion, the keys to her huge improvement were:
    1) she religiously used ice therapy after every training session, and
    2) we increased her training volume using a pure Soviet System.

Dynamic and kinematic structure of the most effective exercises to develop maximum strength, speed strength, resistance strength and explosive strength

The lift is divided into phases. This is true for both the snatch and clean and jerk. The above figure shows the kinematics of the lift. It also shows the phases of the lift separated by vertical lines (the final phases of recovery are not shown). The phases of the snatch and clean and jerk will be separately detailed on the following pages.

First, let's discuss what can be learned from the figure: the relationships between force and velocity.

The minimum force occurs as the bar passes the knees. The maximum force occurs as the athlete starts their final extension of the pull. Interestingly, velocity peaks at the top of the pull while the force almost drops rapidly, reaching zero shortly thereafter.

Physically, the lifter is applying a maximal force, which then causes the bar to reach maximum velocity. As the bar velocity is about to peak, the lifter is going under the bar. As the lifter turns over and goes under the bar, the force drops to zero. This physically makes sense as the bar is still travelling upward, while the lifter's body is no longer imparting force on the bar; in a sense, the lifter is in free fall.

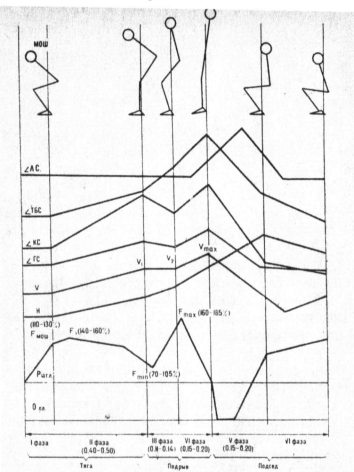

Рис. 12. Фазовая структура основных действий в рывке (по В. И. Фролову, 1976); F — величина опорной реакции, О$_{пл}$ — нулевая линия, Р$_{атл}$ — уровень веса атлета, H — высота подъема штанги, V — скорость подъема, ∠ КС ТБС, ГС, ЛС — углы сгибания в коленном, тазобедренном, голеностопном и локтевом суставах.

Figure 7 - Phases of the lift with velocity, force, and acceleration. Excerpt from Medvedev's book to Dr. Herrera, photo by Dr. Herrera (Medvedev, 1985)

Phases of the Snatch

The snatch is composed by ACTIONS, PERIODS, and PHASES (Lukashov 1972 and Miulberg 1988). These are scientifically accepted terms which enable lifters and coaches to share ideas with other coaches and lifters from around the world. Note that these terms reflect the fact that a perfect snatch is one continuous motion, particularly the pull.

The figure below shows the structure of the snatch. Each action is broken down into phases and periods. The figure shows these periods and phases labeled on a snatch sequence of a Risto Sports lifter on his way to medaling at the American Open in 2013. It is important to recognize that the number of phases in **Figure 7**, the Soviet figure, match those in **Figure 8**. **Figure 7** only shows the velocity and force up until phase 7, the shock absorption. **Figure 9** nicely applies the periods and phases from **Figure 8** on a real world lifter.

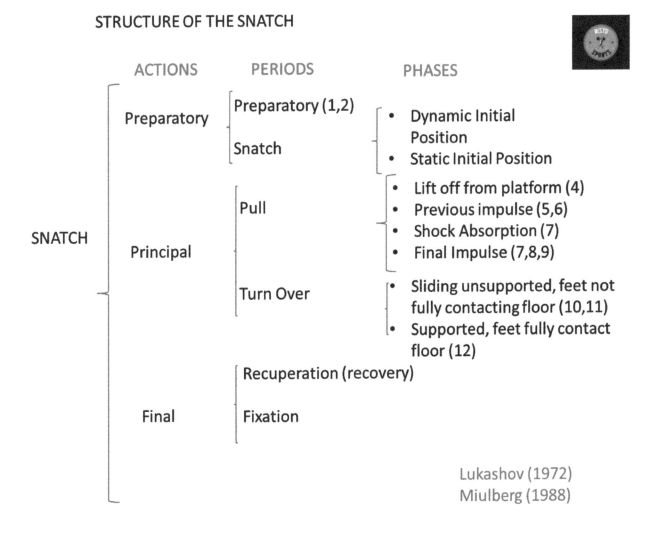

Figure 8 - Actions, Periods, and Phases of the snatch (Perez, Unknown)

The preparatory action focuses on the start position of the lifter and ends when the bar lifts-off the platform. The start position can be either dynamic or static. A dynamic position involves the lifter moving their hips into the bar and giving a final impulse with which to help initiate lift-off. A static start involves lowering oneself down into the start position, flexing the muscles of the legs, then going into the lift-off. Some see the dynamic as more beneficial as a pulse of energy is being transferred from the lifter by quickly lowering their hips down and forward then straight into the lift off motion. It is, however, an effort of precision and it is very easy for the lifter to mistime this motion and throw phase 4 off. Lifters like Nikolai Peschalov have used this to win Olympic Medals. The static position enables the lifter to stretch down into their hamstrings, storing energy similarly to how a compressed spring stores energy. Provided the lifter does not linger too long in this position, this can act as a spring force which enables a stronger lift-off. This position also tends to be more repeatable, leading to fewer technical errors, as the lifter is not timing the cranking motion of the hips and upper leg with the start of the lift. Naim Suleymanoglu, one of the most successful weightlifters of all time, used a static start position.

The next portion of the snatch is the "principal action". It is aptly named as it contains the pull and turnover periods of the snatch- both which can make or break a lift. These are further broken down into the following phases: lift-off, previous impulse, shock absorption, final impulse. The lift-off describes the bar coming off the floor. The previous impulse, shock absorption, and final impulse is referring to energy transmitted to the bar prior to passing the knees, passing the knees, and then final burst of energy (or impulse) transmitted before the bar turns over.

The turn-over period commences imediately after the pull. This includes the phases 10 and 11 where the bar is traveling upward, unmsupported by the lifter, which enables the lifter to slide their feet out. This is somewhat similar to a baseball player throwing a ball straight into the air, where the ball, like the bar, has enough energy imparted into it, that it can travel upward without any further action from the athlete. The only difference, here, being that the lifters hands are still connected to the bar, even though they impart negligible force on it in this phase. In phase 13, the feet are fully contacting the floor, and the lifter has caught the bar. The feet are now creating a normal force against the platform, and the lifter is fully supporting the bar in an overhead squat position.

The "final" action consists of the recovery and fixation periods. These periods describe the athlete standing-up with the bar and holding it overhead for the down signal.

Figure 9 - Snatch sequence labeled with structure of the snatch of Risto Lifter Elio Guerra, photo licensed by Hookgrip

Again, the clean and jerk follows similar phases and periods as the snatch. Phases for the jerk are also constructed. The actions of the clean follow the same pattern as the snatch.

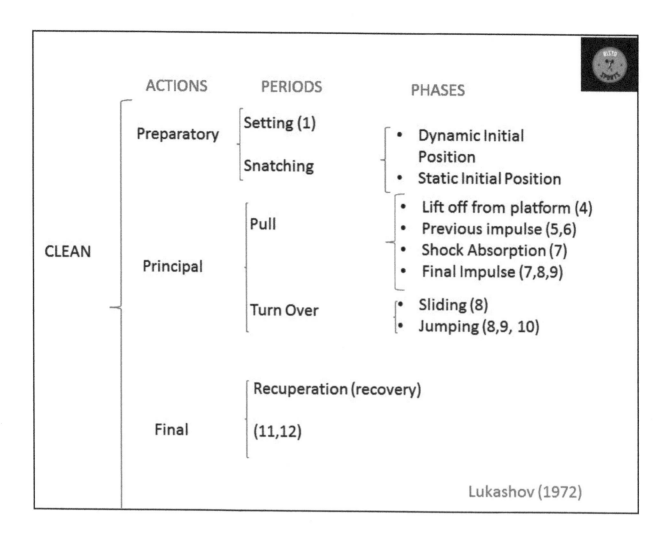

Figure 10 - Actions, Periods, Phases of the clean (Perez, Unknown)

Just like the clean and the snatch, the jerk also has Preparatory, Principal, and Final actions. As shown in **Figure 10**, the periods are also similar. The prelude period, though, is markedly different from the pull periods of the snatch and clean. The prelude period consists of semi-flexion, breaking, and thrust phases. The Semi-flexion phase describes the athlete dipping downward with the bar by bending their knees. The breaking phase is when the athlete changes direction with their dip- the point where they stop descending. The thrust phase is when the athlete explodes out of the dip and moves the bar upward.

The next phase describes the athlete sliding under the bar into a split (for some lifters, a squat or power jerk position), then supporting the bar overhead. Just like the snatch, it completes with a recovery and fixation period, composed of the lifter bringing their feet together and standing-up with the bar fully overhead. **Figure 12** shows the actions, periods, and phases on an elite Cuban lifter competing, at the time, for Risto Sports.

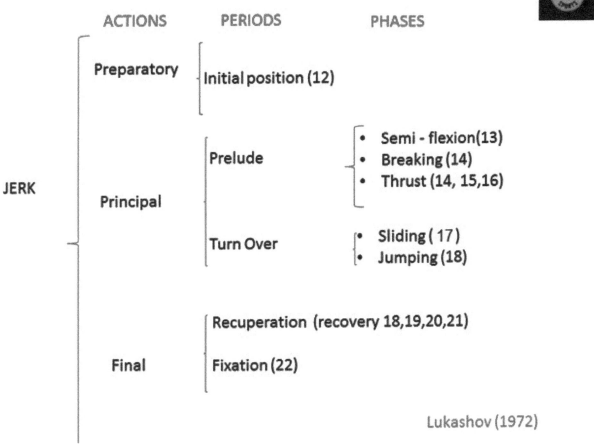

Figure 11 - Actions, Periods, and Phases of the Jerk (Lukashov 1972) (Perez, Unknown)

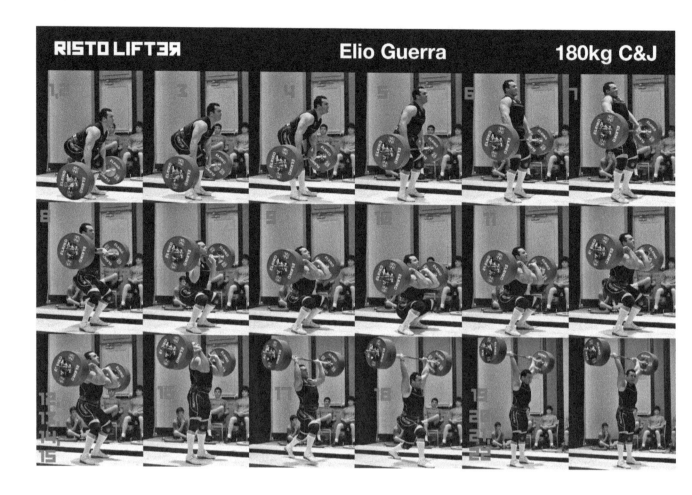

Figure 12 - Phases of the clean and jerk, demonstrated by Risto lifter Elio Guerra, Photo licensed by Hookgrip

Executing exercises with a different rhythm to increase results

In practice, 60% of the best Soviet lifters considered it useful to execute the exercises of squats, pulls, and bench press with a slow rhythm every 7-10 days at the end of their training sessions (Hererra, 2012). In particular, the pull could be done with a slow return. Unlike the snatch and clean and jerk, the return of the pull, squat, and bench press can be executed at a different rhythm when they are used as strength exercises and not technical exercises. Whereas, it would be highly detrimental to execute technical exercises, like the snatch and clean and jerk, at different rhythms, as the goal in training is to make technique, including speed, as repeatable and reflex like as possible.

In terms of varying rhythm of strength exercises, the Soviets completed a study on varying the rhythm of the squat and increase in the athlete's squat personal record. **Table 4** shows the results. The subject lifters were placed into 5 different groups. Each group executed the squat at a different rhythm. The column at the far right shows the actual average kilograms the group's squat increased plus or minus the standard deviation (in other words, the spectrum of improvement

Experiment performed by Lelokov to increase squat strength		
Group	Rhythm of execution	Increase of Strength Kg
1	Fast	9±0.9
2	Medium	16.3±0.5
3	Slow	9.5±0.8
4	Very Slow	11.2±1.1
5	Varied	22.2±0.6

was given for each squat group).
Table 4 - Optimal rhythm of the squat exercise (Lelokov)

As seen in the above table, varying the speed of squats had the best improvement in strength. Squatting with a fast rhythm had the lowest improvement. Varying rhythm also had the second lowest standard deviation, meaning the results had less variation. This meaning athletes in this group were less spread apart, or more similar results, than in a group with higher standard deviation.

To practically apply squatting in different rhythms, the lifter can either schedule a change in squat pace every 7-10 days , or simply change squat rhythm between repetitions or even sets during daily training. If the athlete finds it too difficult to modulate the rhythm of their squats, then they could simply apply a medium speed. Whereas, medium speed was found to be the second most effective method for improving squat results; it also had the lowest standard deviation of the 5 rhythms tested.

Creating a Training program

Training with weights loading and its meaning according to period of training

Key Definitions:
- **Organism**: the subject or, in this case, the athlete
- **Training load**: It's the group of stimuli that causes a chain reaction of the functional systems in the organism. The effectivity of the training load is valued by the deepness and duration of changes in the organism (Hererra, 2012)
- **Repetitions**: Each lift completed for a particular exercise. Abbreviated as "reps"
- **Set**: a group of repetitions completed without significant rest in between
- **Volume (Repetitions, Kg lifted, kilometers, kilocalories)**: This is the indicator of quantity of stimuli
- **Intensity**: The indicator of Quality of stimuli or level of difficulty, determined, basically, by the maximum result (Hererra, 2012). Whereas, intensity is calculated as the percent of the athlete's maximum result
- **Personal Record**: the athlete's best result in any lift. Also known as their "max" or "PR"
- **Max out (maxxing-out)**: when the athlete attempts to lift 100% or more of their personal record in training

Intensity Zones
Before discussing program design, intensity zones must be defined. Intensity is segregated into seven zones in which the lifter works.

Zone number	Intensity (percentage of personal record)
1	50-59%
2	60-69%
3	70-79%
4	80-489%
5	90-100%
6	100-110%
7	+110 %

Table 5 - Intensity Zones (Hererra, 2012)

Table 5 shows the different intensity zones established by the Soviets. The Soviets divided intensity into seven zones, through empirical studies. When coaches program, we talk about amount of work done in an intensity zone. As defined above, an intensity zone is a range of percentage of a best lift. For example, intensity zone 3 is 70-79%. If a lifter's best lift is 100kg, then any lifts done from 70kg to 79kg would be work done in intensity zone 3. Medvedev followers look primarily at the number of repetitions or "volume" completed in an intensity zone. As we will see with mesocycles , macrocycles, and microcycles, depending on which cycle the lifter is in, the lifter will do most work in a particular intensity zone. These cycles and volume are discussed in the following sections.

It is important to observe that intensity under 50% is not represented on this chart. Specifically, the Soviets do not count repetitions done at less than 50% of a lifter's PR towards the training cycle's volume. For example, if a lifter's best snatch is 200kg, warm-ups done with the bar up to 100kg are not counted as work done towards the lifter's training program. Nevertheless, work with the bar and light weight should always be done before a training session for the purposes of safely and effectively warming-up, including for improving technique.

Training cycle design

The programming of a weightlifter's training is done methodically, purposefully, and scientifically. The weightlifter's program is designed in yearly blocks, then broken down in to blocks of 3 months, then broken down further into blocks of a week at a time. Workouts where the weightlifter attempts greater than 95% of their best lifts are planned events.

Volume and intensity are the two key parameters in programming design. Programming is a delicate balance of volume and intensity.

Figure 13 shows the cyclic nature of volume and intensity. As we progress through this chapter, the dance these two parameters play in creating a champion's program will become more clear.

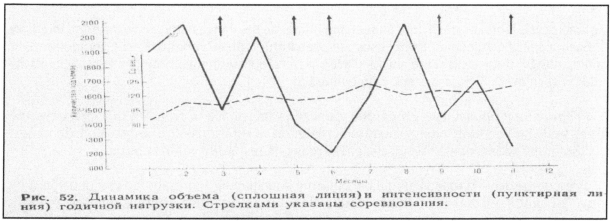

Рис. 52. Динамика объема (сплошная линия) и интенсивности (пунктирная линия) годичной нагрузки. Стрелками указаны соревнования.

Figure 13 - Volume and intensity by month. Dashed line is volume (number of repetitions), solid line is intensity (%). Chart is from Dr Hererra's personal copy of Medvedev (Medvedev, 1985)

Cycles and Intensity

The cyclical nature of volume and intensity is an output of the cycles detailed below in Table 6. The four cycles shown determine when and how volume and intensity are increased and decreased.

Term	Definition	Comments
Olympic Cycle	The 4 years leading up to the Olympics	The Olympic quad or quadrennium
Macrocycle	The plan for the quarter- 3 months or 12 weeks	Also, known as a "12 week program" where 3 months is equivalent to 12 weeks.
Mesocycle	The plan for 1 month out of the macrocycle	
Microcycle	The plan for the week	One week out of the mesocycle. This cycle is further broken down into individual training days

Table 6 - Cycles of the Training Year

Coaches program by working from defined start points towards defined control points (ie major competitions). The end of the Olympic cycle determines the start of the first macrocycle for the next Olympic cycle. From there, mesocycles are then planned. Then, mesocycles are broken down into weeks or microcycles. This is a form of functional decomposition, where we start from a large chunk like macrocycles then break them down into smaller chunks such as quarters of a year, then weeks, then days, then training sessions.

The macrocycle is broken down into phases that influence the dance between volume and intensity to reach a specific objective. The phases are preparatory, pre-competitive, and competition. In training design, these phases are always placed in the aforementioned order, as they sequentially build on each other. They are specifically defined as:

Preparatory phase: The preparatory phase is the phase of training that prepares the lifter's body for handling maximal loads. It creates an adaptation of the body to high demands. It is the first 7 weeks of a 12 week cycle. There is one test point in this phase.

Pre-competitive phase: This phase continues preparing the body for competition. The body can handle increased intensity while volume is maintained. There is one test point in this phase.

Competitive phase: This is the final phase of training before a competition. The volume is decreased and the intensity increases to its greatest. There are 2-3 test points in this phase in which the lifter is prepared to max out.

Table 7 shows each of the phases by week of the macrocycle. Per table 7, each phase includes test points– also known as "controls" or "max-outs". During week 7, the lifter can go up to 100% and should not necessarily seek to exceed their PR. Week 9 the lifter may go above 100 %; week 9 contains the first test point of the cycle where new PR's are sought. It is even more pertinent that the lifter exceed their PR by Week 12. During Week 12, the lifter must hit as a high a max as possible. In effect, the coach should design the program for a lifter to compete at an important competition in week 12 of their cycle.

Phase of training	Week ranges	Intensity	Test points
Preparatory phase	Weeks 1-7	Lowest of the cycle	Week 7, up to 100%
Pre-competitive phase	Weeks 8-10	Medium - High	Week 9, above 100%
Competitive phase	Weeks 11-12	Highest of the cycle	Week 11-12, above 100% Week 12, highest lifts of the cycle, new personal records must be attempted

Table 7 - Training Phase by week and control points

Strategic planning, Getting the most out of the training cycle

By planning in 12 week cycles, the athlete's body will adapt to peak at more predictable times. This is a huge advantage over other training systems, because the coach and/or athlete can predict when the athlete will be ready to hit a big Personal Record. By modulating the volume and intensity, we can goad the athlete's body into hitting 100% or more 3 to 4 times in a cycle at fairly known times. Hence, it is imperative that the cycle is designed around key competitions.

The goal of the training cycle is to hit new personal records at the athlete's most important competition. Thus, before planning the start of the cycle, it is important that the coach understands which competitions are the most important competitions of the year for their athlete. The coach must know which competition is the most important of the year for the athlete, then understand which competitions are of secondary importance. They should also look at competition schedules to find smaller practice competitions.

For example, a lifter looking to compete at a World Championship would plan their cycle around the World Championships as the maximal point in the year. Then, they would work backwards and program around the key qualifying competitions for the World Championships, such as the National Championships. Further, the athlete might need to post a qualifying total at a local competition to compete at nationals, these meets could fall in weeks where the athlete is doing above 90% such as week 7.

The most important competitions should fall at the end of each 12 week cycle and smaller warm-up competitions occurring towards the beginning of the cycle. An underlying assumption here is: it is important to compete as much as possible when the intensity level is planned to be over 95%. This is due to psychological benefits of competing often and the pragmatic viewpoint that PR's should not be left in the training hall on YouTube videos. Figure 8 highlights the max out points in the mesocycles, and it also shows the general intensity ranges of the microcycles.

The way this works out practically is that the most important meet of the year will fall on week 12 of the final mesocycle of the year. Secondary meets, such as qualifiers for the primary competition, should also be programmed around such that they fall on week 12 of prior mesocycles.

Within each of these mesocycles, it is customary to compete at least 2 times before week 12- usually week 7 and 10. By doing so, the athlete and coach will get the most out of their pre-competitive and competitive phases of training. Hence, many times, a coach will schedule either a test meet prior or a training camp to the actual competition. Figure 8 highlights weeks in yellow where the lifter is expected to do at least 100%. If the lifter looks in good condition, they can attempt over 100% in these weeks on the last day of the week.

Another very important thing to observe in **Table 8** is that the 3 primary exercises- snatch, clean and jerk, and squat- do not always have the same intensity zones worked. In some microcycles, both the snatch and clean and jerk are maxxed. Some weeks, the squat and clean and jerk are maxxed.

	Mesocycle I			Mesocycle II			Mesocycle III	
	Snatch	60 % - 80%		Snatch	60% - 87%		Snatch	65% - 105%
Micro I	C&J	65 % - 80%	Micro I	C&J	60% - 87%	Micro I	C&J	65% - 105%
Week 1	Squat	60% - 85%	Week 5	Squat	60% - 85%	Week 9	Squat	65% - 83%
	Snatch	60 % - 85%		Snatch	70% - 95%		Snatch	60% - 90%
Micro II	C&J	60% - 85%	Micro II	C&J	60% - 97%	Micro II	C&J	65 % - 90%
Week 2	Squat	55% - 85%	Week 6	Squat	50% - 100%	Week 10	Squat	50% - 100%
	Snatch	60% - 90%		Snatch	60% - 100%		Snatch	60% - 90%
Micro III	C&J	65 % - 90%	Micro III	C&J	60% - 100%	Micro III	C&J	60% - 90%
Week 3	Squat	50% - 90%	Week 7	Squat	60% - 95%	Week 11	Squat	60% - 100%
	Snatch	65% - 92%		Snatch	70% - 95%		Snatch	65% - 105%
Micro IV	C&J	65% - 92%	Micro IV	C&J	60% - 100%	Micro IV	C&J	65% - 105%
Week 4	Squat	65% - 95%	Week 8	Squat	60% - 100%	Week 12	Squat	65% - 85%

Table 8 -Range of intensity for macrocycle, including its mesocycles and microcycles, highlighted cells are control points

It is common to see videos of lifters from countries with highly organized and centralized training programs to conduct a training camp for the final team selection for major championships. For example, a country like Colombia may have a training camp a month before the World Championships. At the end of the camp, they would have a test competition to select the final team. It is expected that the athletes selected to the team would be able to max out again at the primary competition because the athlete would be at the end of their competitive phase.

Volume

As we have discussed intensity and segments of the macrocycle, the next piece of the programming equation is volume. The program is conceived by setting a goal for the total volume of the macrocycle.

Again, as one macrocycle is a quarter of a year of training, then the volume of the macrocycle is the number of repetitions that the lifter will complete for the entire quarter year. From there, the coach will decide how to spread the volume over each mesocycle. Then within each mesocycle, the coach spreads the volume over each microcycle. Again, this is a form of functional decomposition.

The volume for the macrocycle is split over the 4 mesocycles in a sinusoidal fashion-- it goes up one mesocycle, then down the next. This was demonstrated in Figure 13 (Page 27). At the mesocycle level, the amplitude of this variation-mesocycle to mesocycle – is less than the

Photo 3 - Gwendolyn Rojas competing at the 2015 Kazakhstan Youth National Championships. She is the only American to ever have this honor to compete at a Kazakh Nationals as a guest lifter. She trains at Risto Sports using the Soviet System. Photo by Gwendolyn Sisto.

variation microcycle to microcycle. The highest volume mesocycle is, typically , at the beginning of the macrocycle. That being said, remember to program around the major competition goals of the year, as, just like intensity, the volume is decomposed with the lifter's goals in mind.

As mentioned above, the mesocycle is broken into 3 phases; the phases with lower intensity will see higher cumulative volume. The Preparatory phase will account for the most volume in the mesocycle, with volume reducing through the pre-competitive and competitive phases as intensity increases.

Microcycle programming follows similar suit. With in each phase of the mesocycle, the microcycle also varies. For example, microcycles in the preparatory phase will have weeks of higher volume and lower volume. Low volume, lower intensity weeks are usually referred to as de-load weeks. Like the mesocycle, the waves and undulations of volume and intensity continue from microcycle to microcycle, with the lowest volume and highest intensity weeks occurring in the competitive phase. Further, with in each microcycle, even on de-load weeks, the intensity should follow the following pattern: the first day of the week is the lowest percent of max for the week, volume drops mid-week, and the highest percent of max lifts are done the last day of the week with moderate to higher volume.

The decomposition of the volume described above is tailored to the lifter's needs. The volume is further spread across core exercises also to strengthen the lifter. The suite of exercises also changes as the program progresses from preparatory phase to competitive phase.

Example of how to calculate total volume

Now that we have discussed volume, it is important that we know how to calculate it. **Table 9** shows a sample program. It shows how to calculate volume. It is based on a lifter, for simple purposes, who has a 100kg maximum lift. The particular lift or exercise does not matter, as this calculation is valid for finding the training volume for any exercise.

Indicators of training load, for an athlete with a maximum total of 100kg							
Load	(50 Kg/4)	(65 Kg/3)2	(75 Kg/3)	(82 Kg/3)2	(85 Kg/2	(90 Kg/1)2	Total.
Reps	4	3 x 2=6	3	3 x 2=6	2	2 x1=2	23
Kilos	50x4=200	65x6=390	75x3=225	82x685=2170	85x2=170	90x2=180	1657
Medium weight	1657kg ÷ 23reps = 72						
Medium relative intensity	100 kg=100% of maximum 72/100 = I.M.R.72%						

Table 9 - Example for calculating Total Volume.

The total repetitions are calculated simply by multiplying the reps in a set by the number of sets at each subsequent weight, then summing across. In the example above, there were 23 total reps in the program.

Next, the total kilograms lifted are calculated the same way. Simply take the weight value and multiply it by the number of reps by the number of sets done at each weight. Then we sum across the row which says "kilos" and arrive at 1657kg lifted in total.

The "medium weight" is found by dividing the total kilos lifted by the total reps. In this example, we arrive at 72.

Next, we find the relative medium intensity by dividing the medium weight by the max for the lifter. Again, this method works for any exercise- snatch, clean and jerk, jerk, squat, etc. Depending on the mesocycle and the lifter, the coach will aim for a different relative medium intensity value.

How to spread the volume, using a simple example

First set a goal for the repetitions for the macrocycle.
 • For simplicity sake, let's use 3000 repetitions or a total loading of 3000 repetitions (this is not
      a realistic number).
 • This is all repetitions of all exercises added together.

Then, divide the repetitions by the number of mesocycles – which is 3.

   3000/ 3 = 1000

For a goal of 3000 repetitions in total, in a macrocycle, there should be about 1000 repetitions in the mesocycle.

Next, determine if you want to skew the load towards one mesocycle or another.

From the preceding sections, we know it is desirable to do more volume in the preparatory phase, and less in the competitive phase. Again, for simplicity purposes, move 500 repetitions out of the competitive phase into the pre-competitive phase.

This would yield three mesocycles like this:

   Preparatory phase: 1500 repetitions
   Pre-competitive phase: 1000 repetitions total
   Competitive phase: 500 repetitions

Next, you will need to split the repetitions week by week. Let's take the pre-competitive phase as an example. There are 4 weeks in the pre-competitive phase. Dividing the volume by 4 we get:

   1000/4 =250 repetitions

As you learned earlier in this book, there are de-loading weeks and that volume should be varied sinusoidally. So, you could skew volume away from deload weeks, about every other week. Using a simple example, a pattern could look something like this:

Week 5 350 repetitions

Week 6 200 repetitions

Week 7 150 repetitions - Lowest volume week as lifter goes up to 100% in both snatch and C&J (Table 8)

Week 8 300 repetitions

Next, you will have to go week by week and spread the volume over each day. Let's use week 7, the max out week as an example. If the lifter trains 6 days per week, then the load per day should be about:

Week 7 total volume/ number of training days per week

150/ 6= 25 repetitions

In this example, we would start from 25 repetitions per day and skew it based on intensity variation and keeping a sinusoidal pattern. As you may have learned from the "Kazakhstan Weightlifting System for Elite athletes" (Ivan Rojas, 2015), the highest intensity is in the beginning and end of the week. So, the volume might be spread something like this:

Day 1: 25 repetitions

Day 2: 33 repetitions

Day 3: 23 repetitions

Day 4: 17 repetitions

Day 5: 30 repetitions

Day 6: 22 repetitions

The repetitions used in the above example are far lower than a typical cycle for a competitive lifter. They are used to illustrate an example using easily manipulated numbers.

To get a more realistic sense of how to spread the volume while varying intensity, then review the sample programs at the end of this book. These programs are real macrocycles with realistic repetition counts.

Selecting the right number of training sessions per week in modern American Society

The Soviet training methods pre-dating Medvedev's and Vorobiev's work were created to help make soldiers out of farmers. Therefore, the Soviet System was created with the same mentality and can be applied to any level of training. The programming is simply adjusted to the athlete's training level.

Before embarking on writing a training program for your lifter, first, establish the level of the lifter if:

1a.- Master, Beginner or Recreational lifter- Most Masters depending on fitness level, someone who is starting to lift and lifters who plan to only compete locally.

1b.- Intermediate or more competitive lifter- competes locally with fair results, and has not, yet, qualified to a major national event

1c.- Advanced- competes at major national competitions with fair results

In cases, 1a and 1b, there is more flexibility in the training to increase results. Results tend to come more easily and more rapidly in the earlier skill levels of training.

The number of training sessions selected for 1a and 1b lifters is more based on social factors then capabilities:

1A's: The number of days per week recommended for 1a are 3-4 days per week, with 1 session per day. They can, certainly, train 5-6 days per week, yet, most recreational lifters would burn out or resent training more than 4 times per week in modern American society. The majority of Master lifters will fall into this category. However, Master lifters with a very high level of fitness who also compete on a senior or "open" level may categorize themselves as 1b or 1c based on their competition results.

1B's: It is recommended at least 4 days a week for this group, with 1 session per day. If they are really dedicated to qualifying for a major national event, then bump the days up to 5 to 6, with maybe one day per week that they do a double session. Again, if weightlifting is not their sole focus, then more than 5 days a week may cause resentment

If the lifter is a 1c, or advanced, and is serious about improving, then they should strive for 6 days per week. It is important to know if the lifter has any activities in their personal life that can affect number of training sessions the lifter can do per week. The coach must determine if the lifter falls into any of these categories:

A - If lifter works, studies, has a family and lifts

B - If lifter works or studies and lifts

C - If lifter works or studies part time and lifts

D - If lifter only lifts

This is salient as the training program and the managing of the load should be according time availability of the lifter and their actual situation. Case D, for example, is the ideal case where the lifter can completely arrange their life around training. Lifters who only train for a living should train 6 days a week, and it is best if they can do at least 8-10 training sessions per week. Some full time lifters report doing even up to 12 sessions per week.

Certainly, in cases A, B and C, it is possible for the lifter to organize their schedule to lift 6 days per week; it will, however, be less likely that they can do more than 6-8 sessions per week.

If the coach wants the lifter to succeed, then they must be realistic about the true number of sessions and days per week that the lifter can train. Likewise, it is the responsibility of the lifter to be open and honest about how many sessions and days per week they can train. The lifter must commit to a set number of training days per mesocycle and must have the discipline to stick to the agreed upon schedule.

Likewise, in the appendix of this book, we have included sample programs for 3, 4, 5, and 6 day per week for a full mesocycle. In all cases, the soviet system can be used for any skill level.

Organizing a training log

The daily training should be recorded in a log. It is of utmost importance to keep a record such that athletes and coaches can see progress and understand total repetitions. A sample training log is on the next page.

Data that should be entered by the lifter is the date, bodyweight, heartbeat, and the lifter should note any missed lifts directly on the log. The training log otherwise assumes that all lifts were successful. The lifter may even want to make notes when exercises felt particularly easier than normal, or if they felt they had a breakthrough.

All other information such as the lifter's name, the cycle information , the percentages, repetitions, best recorded lifts, average weight, tonnage, and average intensity zone should be entered by the coach.

It is important to note the Macro, Meso, and Microcycle number and date of training. This will make it easy for the lifter or coach to look back on training cycles and do a comparative analysis. For example, if a lifter is making less than 90% of their lifts for a given micro cycle, it can be useful to look at percentage of completed lifts for the same microcycle of the previous macrocycle. The coach can compare whether the lifter struggled in the same microcycle previously, and, then, they can alter their approach.

Training log				
Name:_____. **Macrocycle** ___. **Mesocycle**___. **Microcycle** ____ **Date**_____				
Body weight Start_____ **Finish**_____ **Time, Start**_____ **Finish** _____				
Heart beat start_____ **Finish**_____ **Best results. Snatch.** <u>80Kg</u> **C&J** <u>95</u> **Kg B. Squat.**<u>130 Kg</u>				
Exercise program	**Rep.**	**Ton**	**Pm**	**IMR**
1-.Power snatch (45 Kg/3)2; (50 Kg/3)2; 55Kg/3; (60 Kg/3)3; (62 Kg/3)2	30	1647	54.9 kg	68.6%
2- .Jerk from rack(55Kg/3)2; 60 Kg/3; (65 Kg/3)2; (70Kg/3)3; (72 Kg/3)2	30	1962	65.4 kg	62.1%
3-.Front squat(65 Kg/5)3;(7 0Kg/4)3; (75Kg/3)4	39	2715	69.6 kg	73.2%
4-.Snatch pull(70Kg/3)2; (75Kg/3)2	12	870	72.5 kg	90.6%
5-. Light jog	P.F.G. 15 min. Aerobic			
6-.25 box jumps	P.F.E. 25 jumps.			
General of training	111	7194	64.8	----
Obs.				

Table 10 - Sample Training log (Herrera 2012)

Adjusting the individuals training plan

Missing lifts
During a cycle, it is expected that a lifter will miss some lifts. Usually, lifts missed behind are counted as lifted during training, and lifts missed out-front or otherwise are considered true misses in training. The lifter, for safety reasons, is also not expected to save lifts in training. The coach should be concerned, though, if the lifter misses more than 10% of their lifts for a given week.

Approaches the coach can take for greater than 10% misses:

- Document in which exercises the lifter had the misses
- Review bodyweight metrics. Loss in more than a kilo per week can be a sign of insufficient recovery.
  ⇒ Countermeasure: Improve diet and recovery methods, see methods in previous chapters.
- Review what number for PR's the percentages were taken off of. If the lifter provided an inflated PR number for either the snatch, clean and jerk, or squat, it can make the program unsuccessful
  ⇒ Countermeasure: adjust max , recalculate percentage of max's
  ⇒ Countermeasure: ensure that the max being used is the original max used to calculate percentages initially for the cycle.
- Ensure athlete is reporting any injuries
  ⇒ Countermeasure: seek medical care
- Check technique. Determine whether the lifter's technique has drifted.
  ⇒ Countermeasure: Add 30 min of technical work with the bar at beginning of session
- If all the above seems normal, then
  ⇒ Countermeasure: consider dropping the intensity by a few percent while keeping the repetitions the same.
  - It is always recommended to lower the intensity, first, before lowering the volume.
  - When lifters are missing lifts, never lower the volume without lowering the intensity. This is to keep the lifter safe!
- If all the above are done, then
  ⇒ Countermeasure: lower the volume

Again, the program is adjusted based on metrics. If a lifter is sore and tired and still capable of safely executing greater than 90% of their lifts, then the program may not need to be adjusted. In cases like these, the lifter should improve their recovery methods and utilize some of the many permissible recovery methods covered in prior sections of this book. It is important to managing soreness and fatigue as it can be a negative leading indicator. Note, lifters new to the Soviet system will need time to adapt and are expected to be sore the first mesocycle.

New PR's during the macrocycle
It is of utmost importance that the same maxes or personal records are used to calculate the percentages for the entire Macrocycle. If a lifter hits a new personal record in week 9, for example, the coach is still to use the previous maxes from the beginning of the cycle to finish out the 12 week macrocycle.

Case Study:
Fundamental differences of female lifters from Russia, China and Bulgaria.
Reason for Chinese supremacy

A common misconception is that Bulgarians, in their heyday, maxed-out all the time. Is this true?

In this section, we will look at data comparing the training of China, Bulgaria, and Russia for female lifters in the late 1990's (1998).

Background:
Throughout the 1990's, all three countries were a force in women's lifting. However, in the earlier 1990's Russia had more dominance than the other two countries. By the end of the 90's, China was the undisputed best country in women's weightlifting, sweeping gold medals in almost any weight class they competed in for women. Bulgaria, for its incredibly small size and population, routinely had medalists and/or Champions, which was very impressive considering the size of China and Russia's programs.

One must ask—How was it that China overtook both Russia and Bulgaria?

We can answer this by looking at actual data on the programming methods of these three famed countries.

In **Table 11** (next page), we can see the volume lifters completed in the preparatory and competition phases. The variable "X" indicates the average or mean. The variable "0" indicates the standard deviation or variance. These two variables are listed for all three countries for various training indicators.

Volume of the preparatory and competitive mesocycles of female lifters from Russia, China and Bulgaria.						
Indicators of volume in repetitions.	China		Bulgaria		Russia	
	X	(σ)	X	(σ)	X	(σ)
General total of reps. In all zones	4633	212	4093	139	3333	159
Number of rep. In all exercises with 70+%	2339	131	2279	97	1484	70
Reps with 70%+ (Exercises of Snatch)	508	39	565	37	224	23
Reps with70%+ (Exercises of C&J)	673	71	600	31	240	17
Reps Snatch and C&J	1181	106	1165	64	464	33
Total of snatch pulls	260	21	75	14	270	30
Total reps clean pull	281	25	129	12	238	15
Total reps squats	617	50	910	33	512	27
Reps of pulls and squats.	1158	68	1114	43	1020	47
Sports Mastery (Chart of Starabutsev) Snatch	124±6		107±4.7		72±6.2	

Table 11 - Volume of the competitive and preparatory phases of female lifters from China, Russia, and Bulgaria (Hererra, 2012)

In this time period, Russia had dropped the number of repetitions that its female weightlifters were doing on an annual basis. Meanwhile, China's coaches had increased the number of repetitions. Most of the repetitions were concentrated in the snatch and clean and jerk. The increase in repetitions correlated with China overtaking Russia and Bulgaria.

Table 12 shows something equally interesting. As internet folklore goes, the Bulgarians are rumored to do the highest intensity of all systems. Looking closely at Table 12, the intensity coefficient of the Bulgarian team is only 3% higher than the Chinese intensity coefficient and about the same percent higher than the Russian coefficient. This means that the Bulgarians only do slightly more intensity than Soviet based systems. The difference is not significant, or, rather, the intensities between the systems can be considered to be almost the same.

Upon examining snatch repetitions done at 90% or more, the Chinese actually did more repetitions than the Bulgarians. This is not to contradict the fundamentals of the Soviet system; this is, actually, easily explained by the mesocycle phase. As discussed earlier, In the Soviet system, work in the higher intensity zones increases towards the end of the macrocycle, in the mesocycles covering the pre-competitive and competitive phases. As discussed in **Table 8**, there are 3 weeks where the lifter goes up to or above 100%, and the competitive and pre-competitive phases will see more work in the 70+% intensity zone. In effect, the charts are over competitive and pre-competitive phases where Russian and Chinese lifters would do more repetitions at the higher intensities.

Chart 3. **General indicators of intensity of training**						
Indicators	China		Bulgaria		Russia	
	X (mean)	(σ) (standard deviation)	X	(σ)	X	(σ)
General intensity coefficient	38.2	0.56	39.4	0.7	38.3	0.6
Snatch and C&J intensity coefficient	41.1	0.54	40.3	0.7	40	0.38
Snatch pull intensity coefficient	99.2	2.08	98.1	3.3	107.2	2.75
Clean pull intensity coefficient	95.5	1.19	97	1.6	98.8	1.09
Squat intensity coefficient	100.5	1.04	93.8	1.6	97.5	1.20
Total reps with 90% Snatch and C&J	185	30	105	8	50	11

Table 12 - Intensity of the training of Bulgarian, Chinese, and Russian lifters (Herrera, 2012)

Notes on applicability to other sports

The Soviet system works for anything. It is fundamentally a delicate balance between reps and intensity, as well as work and recovery. To apply this system to another activity, simply replace the exercises with the exercises of the new activity of interest.

Dr Herrera once relayed a story where he applied the Soviet System to managing the workload of a prominent engineer. He indicated that the chief designer of the Russian MiG (Mikoyan), had been suffering deleterious health effects from working too hard (Herrera, 2012). Dr Herrera created a "training program" for the chief designer, whereby the DR varied the chief designer's workload day to day, week to week, similarly to how loading is varied in a weightlifting program. This resulted in positive health effects.

In summary, the principles of the Soviet System can be applied to anything that involves a defined workload to be done over a defined period of time.

Sample Programs

The following chapters are sample 12 week programs or 1 mesocycle. They are divided into 3 to 6 day a week programs. The below section gives guidance on how to read the programs.

Nomenclature- how to read the programs
The following examples show how to understand the nomenclature used in the programs included in this book.

Example 1: Sets by reps
> Snatches 70 (2x3)

The lifter or coach should read this as snatches at 70% of max for 2 sets of 3 repetitions.

Example 2: Power clean and power jerk complexes
> P. Clean + 3PJ   60%(3x1-1) 65%(3x1-2)

This is interpreted as at 60% of max do 1 power clean, 3 power jerks for one set ; at 65% of max do 1 power clean, 3 power jerks for 2 sets.

Example 2A: Power clean and power jerk complexes
> P. Clean + PJ   60%(3x1-1) 65%(3x1-2)

This is interpreted as at 60% of max do 1 power clean, 3 power jerks for one set ; at 65% of max do 1 power clean, 3 power jerks for 2 sets.

Example 3: Reps, only 1 set
> Back Squat 70%x4 80%x3

This is interpreted as back squat 70% of max for 4 reps for 1 set, then back squat 80% of max for 3 reps for 1 set.

Example 4: Back squat plus jerk behind neck
Back Squat +Jerk 45% (2x3)

Interpret as back squat 45% of max 2 sets of 3 reps each in the back squat and jerk. The reps should be done as such, one back squat followed by a jerk, then another back squat followed by a jerk, then followed by another backsquat followed by a jerk.

Example 5: Power Clean, Front squat, power jerk combination
P. clean + front squat + PJ 60% (4x1-2)
Do 1 power clean, 1 front squat, followed by 4 power jerks for 2 sets.

Example 6: Light Jog
The athlete is expected to jog for up to 15 minutes. The jog should be carried out at a leisurely pace. The athlete should not feel any significant muscle fatigue, especially in the legs. It is important for recovery that the athlete abide by these guidelines.

Example 7: Technique work
At the conclusion of some of the training sessions, the phrases "Snatch w bar" and "clean and jerk w bar" are shown. They are abbreviations for "snatch with empty bar" and "clean and jerk with empty bar". These exercises are meant to be purely technical work with the bar.

Gwendolyn Sisto and Ivan Rojas

12 week program

How to do it in a perfect world

In a perfect world the lifter would get up early in the morning (5:00 am or 6:00) and do some stretches, technique with stick, little jogging (6 minutes). The lifter would go back to bed and sleep until 8:30 am and have breakfast around 9:00 am. The first session of the day @ 9:30-10:00 am would be Squats and pulls and abdominal work. Lunch and rest in the afternoon between 4:00 or 5:00 pm the Snatch exercise of the day with 20 minute break after it. The second exercise would be C&J exercise and abdominal work. Supper and sometimes a light session of bodybuilding exercises.

This would require training 6 days per week. One sample macrocycle for a 6 day per week program is included in this book. The days which are shown as single session days, can be split into 2 sessions per day and timed in accordance with the above paragraph.

If you don't live in a perfect world for training, then skip to the next page.

How to do it in America

In America, most weightlifters are not full time athletes. Most have side jobs or full time jobs, even careers. Still, many have been wildly successful in spite of not being able to train as if they lived in a perfect world.

To help those athletes who may not be able to train in a perfect fulltime schedule, we have included several different sample macrocycles that can be applied to any level of athlete.

In this book, we have 4 sets of 12 week programs, a full macrocycle, for the following training arrangements:

- 6 days a week, recommended for elite and international athletes
- 5 days a week for advanced level athletes
- 4 days a week for intermediate athletes
- 3 days a week for recreational athletes (including Beginners and most Masters)

Gwendolyn Sisto and Ivan Rojas

3 days a week program

Week 1	Macrocycle I, Mesocycle I, Microcycle I							
Day 1	1.-Power Snatch	60%(2x3)	65%(2x3)	70%(2x3)				18 reps
	2.-P. Clean & P. Jerk	65%(3x1-2)	70%(3x1-2)	75%(3x1-2)				18 reps
	3.-Back Squat	60%(2x4)	65%(2x4)	70%x3	75%x3	80%(2x3)		28 reps
	4.-Snatch Pull	80%(2x3)	85%(2x3)					12 reps
Day 2	1.- Snatch	70%x3	75%(2x3)	80%x3	83%x3			15 reps
	2.- C & J	65%x3	70%x3	75%(2x3)	80%x3			15 reps
	3.- Front Squat	65%x5	70%(2x4)	80%(2x4)				24 reps
Day 3	1.- Snatch	60%x3	65%(2x3)	70%x3	75%(2x3)	80%(2x3)		24 reps
	2.- C & J	60%x3	65%(2x3)	70%x3	75%(2x3)	80%(2x3)		24 reps
	3.-Back Squat	60%(2x4)	65%x4	70%x3	75%(2x3)	80%(2x3)	85%(2x2)	31 reps
	4.-Snatch Pull	85%(2x2)						31 reps
	5.-Ab work	80%(2x3)	85%(2x3)					12 reps
Obs	221 reps. 57 reps snatch. 57 reps C&J. 83 reps squats. 12 reps pulls.							

Week 2	Macrocycle I, Mesocycle I, Microcycle II							
Day 1	1.- Power Snatch	60%(2x3)	65%(2x3)	70%x3	75%x3			15 reps
	2.- P. Clean+ 3 PJ	65%(3x1-1)	70%(3x1-1)	75%(3x1-1)	80%(3x1-2)			15 reps
	3.- Back Squat	60%(2x5)	65%(2x5)	70%x4	75%x3	80%(2x3)		35 reps
	4.- Snatch pull	85%(2x3)	90%(2x3)					12 reps
Day 2	1.- Snatch	60%x3	65%x3	70%x3	75%x3	80%x3		15 reps
	2.- C & J	60%x3	65%x3	70%x3	75%x3	80%x3		15 reps
	3.- Back Squat	70%(2x4)	75%(2x4)	80%x4	85%(2x3)			26 reps
	4.- Snatch pull	85%(2x3)	90%(2x3)					12 reps
Day 3	1.- Snatch	60%x3	65%(2x3)	70%x3	75%x3	80%x3	85%x2	20 reps
	2.- C & J	55%x3	60%x3	65%x3	70%x3	75%x3	80%x3	
		85%x2						20 reps
	3.- Back Squat	55%x5	60%x5	65%x5	70%x5	75%x4	80%x5	30 reps
		85%x3	90%(2x2)					36 reps
	215 reps. 50 reps snatch. 50 reps C&J. 91 reps squat. 24 reps pulls							

Week 3	Macrocycle I, Mesocycle I, Microcycle III							
Day 1	1.- Power Snatch	60%(2x3)	65% x 3	70%x3	75%x3	80%(2x3)		21 reps
	2.- P Clean+P Jerk	65%(3x1-1)2	70%(3x1-1)	75%(3x1-1)2	80%(3x1-1)2			21 reps
	3.- Back Squat	60%(3x5)	65%(2x5)	70%x4	75%x3	80%(2x3)		38 reps
	4.- Snatch Pull	85%(2x3)	90%(2x3)					12 reps
Day 2	1.- P Snatch below kn	50%(2x3)	55%(2x3)	60%x3	70%x3	75%(2x3)		21 reps
	2.- P Clean+P Jerk	65%(3x1-1)2	70%(3x1-1)	75%(3x1-1)2	80%(3x1-1)2			21 reps
	3.- Back Squat	60%(2x5)	65%(2x5)	70%x4	75%x3	80%x3	85%x3	33 reps
	4.- Snatch Pull	85%(2x3)	90%(2x3)					12 reps
Day 3	1.- Snatch	65%x3	70%(2x3)	75%x3	80%x3	85%x3	90%x2	25 reps
		80%x3	90%x2					
	2.- C & J	55%x3	60%x3	65%x3	70%x3	75% x 3	80%x3	25 reps
		85%x3	80%x2	90%x2				
	3.- Back Squat	50%x5	55%x4	60%x4	65%x4	70%(2x3)	75%x3	36 reps
		80%(2x3)	85%x2	90%x2				
	4.- Snatch Pull	85%(2x3)	90%(2x3)					12 reps
Obs								

Week 4	Macrocycle I. Mesocycle I. Microcycle 3								
Day 1	1.- Power Snatch	65%x3	70%(2x3)	75%x3	80%x3	83%x3			18 reps
	2.- P Clean + 3 P Jerks	65%(3x1-1)	70%(3x1-1)	75%(3x1-2)	80%(3x1-1)	83%(3x1-1)			18 reps
	3.- Back Squat	60%x5	65%(2x5)	70%x5	75%x3	80%x3	83%x3		29 reps
	4.- Snatch Pulls	85%(2x3)	90%(2x3)						12 reps
	5.- Ab work								
	6.- Light jogg	15 minutes							
Day 2	1.- Snatch	65%x3	70%x3	75%x3	80%x3	83%x3			15 reps
	2.- C & J	65%x3	70%x3	75%x3	80%x3	85%x3			15 reps
	3.- Fron Squat	70%(2x5)	75%(2x5)	80%x4	85%(2x3)				30 reps
	4.- Ab work								
Day 3	1.- Snatch	65%x3	70%(2x3)	75%x3	80%x3	85%x3	90%x1	92%x1	20 reps
	2.- C & J	60%x3	65%(2x3)	70%x3	75%x3	80%x3	85%x2	90%x1	
		92%x1							22 reps
	3.- Back Squat	60%x4	65%x4	70%x4	75%x4	80%x3	85%x3	90%x3	
		92%x1	95%x1						29 reps
	4.- Snatch Pulls	85%(2x3)	90%(2x3)						12 reps
Obser	218 reps. 53 reps snatch. 53 reps C&J. 88 reps squat. 24 reps pulls								

Week 5	Macrocycle I, Mesocycle II, Microcycle I						
Day 1	1.- Power Snatch	60%(2x3)	65%x3	70%x3	75%x3	80%(2x3)		21 reps
	2.- P C +3P Jerks	65%(3x1-2)	70%(3x1-1)	75%(3x1-2)	80%(3x1-2)			21 reps
	3.- Back Squats	60%(3x5)	65%(2x5)	70%x4	75%x3	80%x3	83%x3	38 reps
	4.- Snatch Pull	85%(2x3)	90%(2x3)					12 reps
	5.- Ab work							
Day 2	1.- Snatch	65%x3	70%x3	75%x3	80%x3	85%x3	90%x2	17 reps
	2.- C & J	65%x3	70%x3	75%x3	80%x3	85%x3	90%(2x2)	19 reps
	3.- Front Squat	70%(2x4)	75%(2x4)	80%x4	85%(2x3)			26 reps
	4.- Ab work							
Day 3	1.- Snatch	60%x3	65%(2x3)	70%x3	75%x3	80%x3	87%x1	21 reps
		95%(2x1)						
	2.- C & J	60%x3	65%(2x3)	70%x3	75%x3	80%(2x3)	87%x1	24 reps
		95%(2x1)						
	3.- Back Squats	60%(3x5)	65%(2x5)	70%x3	75%x2	80%x2	85%x2	36 reps
		90%x1	95%(2x1)					
	4.- SnatchPull	85%(2x3)	90%(2x3)					12 reps
Obs	247 reps. 59 reps snatch. 64 reps C&J. 100 reps squats. 24 reps pulls.						

Week 6	Macrocycle I. Mesocycle II. Microcycle II						
Day 1	1.- Power Snatch	70%(2x3)	75%x3	80%x3	83%(2x3)		18 reps
	2.- P Clean +3 PJ	60%(3x1-1)	65%(3x1-1)	70%(3x1-1)	80%(3x1-1)		18 reps
	3.- Back Squat	60%x5	65%x5	70%x5	75%x3	80%x3	27 reps
		83%(3x2)					
	4.- Snatch pull	85%(2x3)	90%(2x3)				12 reps
Day 2	1.- Snatch	70%(2x3)	75%x3	80%x3	83%x3		15 reps
	2.- C & J	70%(2x3)	75%x3	80%x3	83%x3		15 reps
	3.- Back Squat	60%x5	65%x5	70%x5	75%(2x3)	80%(2x3)	27 reps
	4.- Snatch pull	85%(2x3)	90%(2x3)				12 reps
Day 3	1.- Snatch	65%x3	70%(2x3)	75%x3	80%x3	85%x2	21 reps
		90%x2	95%(2x1)				
	2.- C & J	65%x3	70%(2x3)	75%x3	80%x2	85%x2	23 reps
		90%x2	95%x1	97%x1			
	3.- Back Squat	50%x4	55%x4	60%x4	65%x4	70%x3	
		75%x3	80%x3	85%x2	90%x1	95%x1	30 reps
		100%x1					
	4.- Snatch pull	85%(2x3)	90%(2x3)				12 reps
Obs	218 reps. 54 reps snatch. 56 reps C&J. 84 reps squats. 24 reps pulls						

Week 7	Macrocycle I, Mesocycle II, Microcycle III						
Day 1	1.-Hang Snatch	60%(2x3)	65%x3	70%x3	75%(3x3)			21 reps
	2.- p Cl + 3 PJ	55%(3x1-1)	60%(3x1-1)	65%(3x1-1)	70%(3x1-1)	75%(3x1-1)	80%(3x1-1)	19 reps
		85%(3x1-2)						
	3.- Back squat	60%x5	65%x5	70%x5	75%x4	80%x4	83%(2x3)	29 reps
	4.- Santch Pulls	90%(2x3)	95%(2x3)					12 reps
Day 2	1.- Snatch	70%2x3	75%x3	80%x3	83%x3			15 reps
	2.- C&J	70%2x3	75%x3	80%x3	83%x3			15 reps
	3.- Back squat	60%x5	65%(2x5)	70%x3	75%x3	80%(2x3)		27 reps
Day 3	1.- Snatch	65%x3	70%x3	75%x3	87%x3	85%x2	90%1	17 reps
		95%x1	100%x1					
	2.- C&J	65%x3	70%x3	75%x3	87%x3	85%x2	90%1	17 reps
		95%x1	100%x1					
Obs	172 reps. 53 reps snatch. 51 reps C&J. 56 reps squats. 12 reps pulls						

Week 8	Macrocycle I, Mesocycle II, Microcycle IV							
Day 1	1.-Power Snatch	70%(2x3)	75%x3	80%x3	83%(3x3)				21 reps
	2.-P Clean+3PJ	60%(3x1-1)	65%(3x1-2)	70%(3x1-1)	75%(3x1-1)	80%(3x1-2)			21 reps
	3.-Back Squat	60%x5	65%x5	70%x5	75%x3	80%x3	85%x3	87%(2x3)	30 reps
	4.- Snatch pull	90%(2x3)	95%(3x3)						12 reps
Day 2	1.- Hang P. Snatch	65%(2x3)	70%x3	75%x3	80%(2x3)				15 reps
	2.- J behind neck	70%x3	75%x3	80%x3	85%x3	87%x3			15 reps
	3.- Back Squat	60%x5	65%x5	70%x3	75%x3	80%(2x3)			22 reps
Day 3	1.- Snatch	65%x3	70%(2x3)	75%x3	80%x3	85%x2	90%x2	95%x1	20 reps
	2.- C & J	50%x3	55%(2x3)	60%x3	65%x3	70%x2	75%x2	80%x2	24 reps
		85%x1	90%x1	95%x1	100%x1				
	3.- Back Squat	50%x4	55%x4	60%x4	65%x4	70%x3	75%x3	80%x3	31 reps
		85%x2	90%x2	95%x1	100%x1				
	4.- Snatch pull	90%(2x3)	95%(2x3)						12 reps
Obs	223 reps. 56 reps snatch. 60 reps C&J. 83 reps squats. 24 reps pulls							

Week 9	Macrocycle I, Mesocycle III, Microcycle I						
Day 1	1.- Snatch	70%(2x3)	75%x3	80%x3	83%(3x3)		21 reps
	2.- C & J	70%(2x3)	75%x3	80%x3	83%(3x3)		21 reps
	3.- Back squat	60%x5	65%x5	70%x5	75%3	80%x3	83%(2x3)	27 reps
Day 2	1.- Hang Snatch	65%(2x3)	70%x3	75%(3x3)			18 reps
	2.- Jerk b neck	65%(2x3)	70%x3	75%(2x3)			15 reps
	3.- Back squat	60%x5	65%x5	70%x4	75%3	80%(2x3)	23 reps
Day 3	1.- Snatch	65%x3	70%x3	75%x2	80%x2	85%x2	90%x2	17 reps
		95%x1	100%x1	105%x1			
	2.- C&J	65%x3	70%x3	75%x2	80%x2	85%x2	90%x2	17 reps
		95%x1	100%x1	105%x1			
	159 reps. 56 reps snatch. 53 reps C&J. 50 reps Squats						

Week 10	Macrocycle I. Mesocycle III. Microcycle II							
Day 1	1.- Power Snatch	60%(2x4)	65%(3x3)	70%x3	75%(2x3)			26 reps
	2.- P Cl + 3 P J	65%(3x1-1)2	70%(3x1-1)2	75%(3x1-1)3	80%(3x1-)2			27 reps
	3.- Back Squats	60%(2x5)	65%(2x5)	70%(2x5)	75%(2x3)	80%x3	83%(2x3)	45 reps
	4.- Snatch Pull	90%(2x3)	93%(2x3)					12 reps
Day 2	1.- Power Snatch	60%x3	65%(2x3)	70%x3	75%(2x3)			18 reps
	2.- Jerk behind neck	60%x5	70%x5	70%(2x3)	75%(2x3)			20 reps
	3.- Front squats	70%(2x5)	75%(2x5)	80%(2x4)	85%(2x4)			43 reps
Day 3	1.- Snatch	60%x3	65%(2x3)	70%x3	75%x3	80%x3	85%x2	25 reps
		87%x1	70%x2	90%(2x1)				
	2.- C&J	60%x3	65%(2x3)	70%x3	75%x3	80%x3	85%x3	25 reps
		87%x2	70%x2	90%(2x1)				
	3.- Back Squats	87%x1	70%x2	90%(2x1)				32 reps
		80%x3	85%x3	90%(2x2)	95%x1	100%x1		
	4.- Snatch Pull	90%(3x3)	93%(2x3)					15 reps
Obs	288 reps.69 reps snatch. 72 reps C&J. 120 reps squats. 27 reps pulls							

Week 11	Macrocycle I. Mesocycle III. Microcycle III									
Day 1	1.- Power Snatch	60%x4	65%(2x3)	70%x3	75%x3	80%x3	83%(2x2)			23 reps
	2.- PCl+3 PJ	65%(3x1-1)	70%(3x1-1)3	75%(3x1-1)	78%(3x1-1)2					24 reps
	3.- Back squat	55%x5	60%x5	65%(2x5)	70%(2x3)	75%x3	80%x3	85%x3		35 reps
	4.- Snatch Pulls	90%(2x3)	93%(2x3)							12 reps
Day 2	1.- Power Snatch	60%x3	65%(2x3)	70%x3	75%(2x3)					18 reps
	2.- Jerk behind neck	65%x5	70%x5	75%(2x3)	78%(2x3)					20 reps
	3.- Front squat	70%x5	75%(2x5)	80%(2x4)	85%x4	90%x2				29 reps
Day 3	1.- Snatch	55%x3	60%x3	65%x3	70%x3	75%x3	80%x2	85%x1	65%x2	22 reps
		92%(2x1)								
	2.- C & J	50%x3	55%(2x3)	60%x3	65%x3	70%x3	75%x2	80%x1	85%x1	24 reps
		90%(2x1)								
	3.- Back squats	45%x5	50%x5	55%x5	60%x4	65%x3	70%x3	75%x3	80%x3	35 reps
		85%x2	90%x2	93%x1	96%x1					
	4.- Snatch Pulls	90%(2x3)	93%(2x3)							12 reps
Obs	254 reps. 63 reps snatch. 68 reps C&J. 99 reps Squat. 24 reps pulls									

Week 12	Macrocycle I. Mesocycle III. Microcycle IV - Competition modeling or control test							
Day 1	1.- Snatch	65%(2x3)	70%x3	75%x3	80%(3x3)			21 reps
	2.- C&J	65%(2x3)	70%x3	75%x3	80%(3x3)			21 reps
	3.- Back Squat	55%x5	60%x5	65%x4	70%x3	75%x3	80%x3	29 reps
		85%x3						
	4.- Snatch pull	90%(2x3)	93%(2x3)					12 reps
Day 2	1.- Hang Snatch	65%x3	70%x3	75%x3	80%(3x3)			18 reps
	2.- Jerk B neck	65%x3	65%x3	70%x3	75%(2x3)			15 reps
	3.- Back Squat	55%x5	60%x5	65%x4	70%x3	75%x3	80%x3	23 reps
Day 3	1.- Snatch	65%x3	70%(2x3)	75%x3	80%x2	85%x1	90%x1	21 reps
		95%x1	70%x2	100%x1	105%x1			
	2.- C&J	65%x3	70%(2x3)	75%x3	80%x2	85%x1	90%x1	21 reps
		95%x1	70%x2	100%x1	105%x1			
Obs	181 reps. 60 reps snatch. 57 reps C&J. 52 reps squats. 12 reps pulls.							

Gwendolyn Sisto and Ivan Rojas

4 days a week program

Week 1	Macrocycle I, Mesocycle I, Microcycle I						
Day 1	1.-Power Snatch	60%(2x3)	65%(2x3)	70%(2x3)			18 reps
	2.-P. Clean & P. Jerk	65%(3x1-2)	70%(3x1-2)	75%(3x1-2)			18 reps
	3.-Back Squat	60%(2x4)	65%(2x4)	70%x3	75%x3	80%(2x3)	28 reps
	4.-Snatch Pull	80%(2x3)	85%(2x3)				12 reps
	5.-Ab work						
	6.-Light jogg	15 minutes					
Day 2	1.- Snatch	70%x3	75%(2x3)	80%x3	83%x3		15 reps
	2.- C & J	65%x3	70%x3	75%(2x3)	80%x3		15 reps
	3.- Front Squat	65%x5	70%(2x4)	80%(2x4)			24 reps
		Ab work					
Day 3	1.-Power Snatch	60%(2x3)	65%x3	70%x3	73%x3		15 reps
	2.- Jerk behind neck	65%(2x3)	70%(2x3)	75%(2x3)			18 reps
	3.- Front Squat	65%x5	70%x4	75%x4	80%(2x3)		19 reps
	4.-Snatch Pull	80%(2x3)	85%(2x3)				12 reps
	5.-Ab work						
Day 4	1.- Snatch	60%x3	65%(2x3)	70%x3	75%(2x3)	80%(2x3)	24 reps
	2.- C & J	60%x3	65%(2x3)	70%x3	75%(2x3)	80%(2x3)	24 reps
	3.-Back Squat	60%(2x4)	65%x4	70%x3	75%(2x3)	80%(2x3) 85%(2x2)	31 reps
	4.-Snatch Pull	85%(2x2)					31 reps
	5.-Ab work	80%(2x3)	85%(2x3)				12 reps
Obs	285 reps. 72 snatch. 75 C&J. 102 squat. 36 pulls						

Week 2	Macrocycle I, Mesocycle I, Microcycle II							
Day 1	1.- Power Snatch	60%(2x3)	65%(2x3)	70%x3	75%x3			15 reps
	2.- P. Clean+ 3 PJ	65%(3x1-1)	70%(3x1-1)	75%(3x1-1)	80%(3x1-2)			15 reps
	3.- Back Squat	60%(2x5)	65%(2x5)	70%x4	75%x3	80%(2x3)		35 reps
	4.- Snatch pull	85%(2x3)	90%(2x3)					12 reps
	5.- Ab work							
	6.- Light jogg	15 minutes						
Day 2	1.- Snatch	60%x3	65%x3	70%x3	75%x3	80%x3		15 reps
	2.- C & J	60%x3	65%x3	70%x3	75%x3	80%x3		15 reps
	3.- Back Squat	70%(2x4)	75%(2x4)	80%x4	85%(2x3)			26 reps
	4.- Snatch pull	85%(2x3)	90%(2x3)					12 reps
	5.- Ab work							
Day 3	1.- Power Snatch	60%x3	65%x3	70%x3	73%(2x3)			15 reps
	2.- Jerk Behind neck	65%(2x3)	70%(2x3)	75%x3	805x3			18 reps
	3.- Front Squat	65%x5	70%x5	75%x5	80%x4			23 reps
	4.- Ab work							
Day 4	1.- Snatch	60%x3	65%(2x3)	70%x3	75%x3	80%x3	85%x2	20 reps
	2.- C & J	55%x3	60%x3	65%x3	70%x3	75%x3	80%x3	
		85%x2						20 reps
	3.- Back Squat	55%x5	60%x5	65%x5	70%x5	75%x4	80%x5	
		85%x3	90%(2x2)					36 reps
	277 reps. 65 snatch. 68 C&J. 120 squat. 24 pulls.							

Week 3	Macrocycle I, Mesocycle I, Microcycle III							
Day 1	1.- Power Snatch	60%(2x3)	65% x 3	70%x3	75%x3	80%(2x3)		21 reps
	2.- P Clean+P Jerk	65%(3x1-1)2	70%(3x1-1)	75%(3x1-1)2	80%(3x1-1)2			21 reps
	3.- Back Squat	60%(3x5)	65%(2x5)	70%x4	75%x3	80%(2x3)		38 reps
	4.- Snatch Pull	85%(2x3)	90%(2x3)					12 reps
Day 2	1.- P Snatch below kn	50%(2x3)	55%(2x3)	60%x3	70%x3	75%(2x3)		21 reps
	2.- P Clean+P Jerk	65%(3x1-1)2	70%(3x1-1)	75%(3x1-1)2	80%(3x1-1)2			21 reps
	3.- Back Squat	60%(2x5)	65%(2x5)	70%x4	75%x3	80%x3	85%x3	33 reps
	4.- Snatch Pull	85%(2x3)	90%(2x3)					12 reps
Day 3	1.- P Snatch	60%x3	65%x3	70%x3	75%(2x3)			15 reps
	2.- Jerk Behind Neck	65%(2x3)	70%(2x3)	75%(2x3)	80%x3			21 reps
	3.- Front Squat	65%(2x5)	70%x5	75%x5	80%(2x5)			30 reps
Day 4	1.- Snatch	65%x3	70%(2x3)	75%x3	80%x3	85%x3	90%x2	25 reps
		80%x3	90%x2					
	2.- C & J	55%x3	60%x3	65%x3	70%x3	75% x3	80%x3	25 reps
		85%x3	80%x2	90%x2				
	3.- Back Squat	50%x5	55%x4	60%x4	65%x4	70%(2x3)	75%x3	36 reps
		80%(2x3)	85%x2	90%x2				
	4.- Snatch Pull	85%(2x3)	90%(2x3)					12 reps
Obs	343 reps. 82 snatch, 88 C&J, 137 squat. 36 pulls.							

Week 4	Macrocycle I. Mesocycle I. Microcycle 3								
Day 1	1.- Power Snatch	65%x3	70%(2x3)	75%x3	80%x3	83%x3			18 reps
	2.- P Clean + 3 P Jerks	65%(3x1-1)	70%(3x1-1)	75%(3x1-2)	80%(3x1-1)	83%(3x1-1)			18 reps
	3.- Back Squat	60%x5	65%(2x5)	70%x5	75%x3	80%x3	83%x3		29 reps
	4.- Snatch Pulls	85%(2x3)	90%(2x3)						12 reps
	5.- Ab work								
	6.- Light jogg	15 minutes							
Day 2	1.- Snatch	65%x3	70%x3	75%x3	80%x3	83%x3			15 reps
	2.- C & J	65%x3	70%x3	75%x3	80%x3	85%x3			15 reps
	3.- Fron Squat	70%(2x5)	75%(2x5)	80%x4	85%(2x3)				30 reps
	4.- Ab work								
Day 3	1.- Power Snatch	60%x3	65%x3	70%x3	75%(2x3)				15 reps
	2.- Jerk behind neck	65%(2x3)	70%(2x3)	75%x3	80%x3				18 reps
	3.- Front Squat	65%x5	70%x5	75%x5	80%(2x5)				25 reps
	4.- Ab work								
Day 4	1.- Snatch	65%x3	70%(2x3)	75%x3	80%x3	85%x3	90%x1	92%x1	20 reps
	2.- C & J	60%x3	65%(2x3)	70%x3	75%x3	80%x3	85%x2	90%x1	
		92%x1							22 reps
	3.- Back Squat	60%x4	65%x4	70%x4	75%x4	80%x3	85%x3	90%x3	
		92%x1	95%x1						29 reps
	4.- Snatch Pulls	85%(2x3)	90%(2x3)						12 reps
Obser	278 reps. 68 snatch. 73 C&J. 113 squat. 24 pull								

Week 5	Macrocycle I, Mesocycle II, Microcycle I						
Day 1	1.- Power Snatch	60%(2x3)	65%x3	70%x3	75%x3	80%(2x3)		21 reps
	2.- P C +3P Jerks	65%(3x1-2)	70%(3x1-1)	75%(3x1-2)	80%(3x1-2)			21 reps
	3.- Back Squats	60%(3x5)	65%(2x5)	70%x4	75%x3	80%x3	83%x3	38 reps
	4.- Snatch Pull	85%(2x3)	90%(2x3)					12 reps
	5.- Ab work							
Day 2	1.- Snatch	65%x3	70%x3	75%x3	80%x3	85%x3	90%x2	17 reps
	2.- C & J	65%x3	70%x3	75%x3	80%x3	85%x3	90%(2x2)	19 reps
	3.- Front Squat	70%(2x4)	75%(2x4)	80%x4	85%(2x3)			26 reps
	4.- Ab work							
Day 3	1.- Power Snatch	60%(2x3)	65%x3	70%x3	75%x3	80%(2x3)		21 reps
	2.- P C +3P Jerks	65%(3x1-2)	70%(3x1-1)	75%(3x1-2)	80%(3x1-2)			21 reps
	3.- Back Squats	60%x5	65%(2x5)	70%x3	75%x3	80%(2x3)	85%(2x3)	33 reps
Day 4	1.- Snatch	60%x3	65%(2x3)	70%x3	75%x3	80%x3	87%x1	21 reps
		95%(2x1)						
	2.- C & J	60%x3	65%(2x3)	70%x3	75%x3	80%(2x3)	87%x1	24 reps
		95%(2x1)						
	3.- Back Squats	60%(3x5)	65%(2x5)	70%x3	75%x2	80%x2	85%x2	36 reps
		90%x1	95%(2x1)					
	4.- SnatchPull	85%(2x3)	90%(2x3)					12 reps
Obs	322 reps. 80 snatch. 85 C&J. 133 squat. 24 pulls						

Week 6	Macrocycle I. Mesocycle II. Microcycle II						
Day 1	1.- Power Snatch	70%(2x3)	75%x3	80%x3	83%(2x3)		18 reps
	2.- P Clean +3 PJ	60%(3x1-1)	65%(3x1-1)	70%(3x1-1)	80%(3x1-1)		18 reps
	3.- Back Squat	60%x5	65%x5	70%x5	75%x3	80%x3	27 reps
		83%(3x2)					
	4.- Snatch pull	85%(2x3)	90%(2x3)				12 reps
Day 2	1.- P Snatch B Kn	70%(2x3)	75%x3	80%x3	83%(2x3)		18 reps
	2.- Jerk b neck	60%x4	65%x4	70%x4	75%x3	80%(2x3)	21 reps
	3.- Front squat	70%(2x5)	75%(2x5)	80%x4	85%x3	87%x3	30 reps
	4.- Snatch pull	85%(2x3)	90%(2x3)				12 reps
Day 3	1.- Power Snatch	70%(2x3)	75%x3	80%x3	83%x3		15 reps
	2.- 1 PC + 3 PJ	60%(3x1-2)	65%(3x1-1)	70%(3x1-1)			15 reps
	3.- Front squat	65%x5	70%x5	75%x5	80%(2x5)		25 reps
	4.- Snatch w bar	5x3					
	5.- C&J w bar	5x3					
Day 4	1.- Snatch	65%x3	70%(2x3)	75%x3	80%x3	85%x2	21 reps
		90%x2	95%(2x1)				
	2.- C & J	65%x3	70%(2x3)	75%x3	80%x2	85%x2	23 reps
		90%x2	95%x1	97%x1			
	3.- Back Squat	50%x4	55%x4	60%x4	65%x4	70%x3	30 reps
		75%x3	80%x3	85%x2	90%x1	95%x1	
		100%x1					
	4.- Snatch pull	85%(2x3)	90%(2x3)				12 reps
Obs	285 reps. 72 snatch. 77 C&J. 112 squat. 24 pulls						

Week 7	Macrocycle I, Mesocycle II, Microcycle III						
Day 1	1.-Hang Snatch	60%(2x3)	65%x3	70%x3	75%(3x3)			21 reps
	2.- p Cl + 3 PJ	55%(3x1-1)	60%(3x1-1)	65%(3x1-1)	70%(3x1-1)	75%(3x1-1)	80%(3x1-1)	19 reps
		85%(3x1-2)						
	3.- Back squat	60%x5	65%x5	70%x5	75%x4	80%x4	83%(2x3)	29 reps
	4.- Snatch pulls	90%(2x3)	95%(2x3)					12 reps
Day 2	1.- Snatch	70%2x3	75%x3	80%x3	83%x3			15 reps
	2.- C&J	70%2x3	75%x3	80%x3	83%x3			15 reps
	3.- Back squat	60%x5	65%(2x5)	70%x3	75%x3	80%(2x3)		27 reps
Day 3	1.- P. Snatch	70%2x3	75%x3	80%x3	83%x3			15 reps
	2.- Jerk bn	70%2x3	75%(2x3)	80%x3	83%x3			18 reps
	3.- Front Squat	65%x5	70%x5	75%x4	80%(2x3)	85%(2x2)		24 reps
	4.- Snatch Bar	3X5						
	5.- C&J Bar	3X5						
Day 4	1.- Snatch	65%x3	70%x3	75%x3	87%x3	85%x2	90%1	17 reps
		95%x1	100%x1					
	2.- C&J	65%x3	70%x3	75%x3	87%x3	85%x2	90%1	17 reps
		95%x1	100%x1					
Obs	217 reps. 68 snatch. 69 C&J. 80 Squat.						

Week 8	Macrocycle I, Mesocycle II, Microcycle IV							
Day 1	1.-Power Snatch	70%(2x3)	75%x3	80%x3	83%(3x3)			21 reps
	2.-P Clean+3PJ	60%(3x1-1)	65%(3x1-2)	70%(3x1-1)	75%(3x1-1)	80%(3x1-2)		21 reps
	3.-Back Squat	60%x5	65%x5	70%x5	75%x3	80%x3	85%x3	87%(2x3)	30 reps
	4.- Snatch pull	90%(2x3)	95%(3x3)					12 reps
Day 2	1.- Hang P. Snatch	65%(2x3)	70%x3	75%x3	80%(2x3)			15 reps
	2.- J behind neck	70%x3	75%x3	80%x3	85%x3	87%x3		15 reps
	3.- Back Squat	60%x5	65%x5	70%x3	75%x3	80%(2x3)		22 reps
Day 3	1.-P Snatch	70%(2x3)	75%x3	80%(2x3)	83% x3			18 reps
	2.-P Clean+3PJ	60%(3x1-1)	65%(3x1-1)	70%(3x1-1)	75%(3x1-1)	80%(3x1-1)	85%(3x1-2)	21 reps
	3.- Front Squat	65%x5	70%x5	75%x5	80%(2x5)			25 reps
Day 4	1.- Snatch	65%x3	70%(2x3)	75%x3	80%x3	85%x2	90%x2	95%x1	20 reps
	2.- C & J	50%x3	55%(2x3)	60%x3	65%x3	70%x2	75%x2	80%x2	24 reps
		85%x1	90%x1	95%x1	100%x1			
	3.- Back Squat	50%x4	55%x4	60%x4	65%x4	70%x3	75%x3	80%x3	31 reps
		85%x2	90%x2	95%x1	100%x1			
	4.- Snatch pull	90%(2x3)	95%(2x3)					12 reps
Obs	287 reps. 74 snatch. 81 C&J. 108 squat. 24 pulls							

Week 9	Macrocycle I, Mesocycle III, Microcycle I						
Day 1	1.- Snatch	70%(2x3)	75%x3	80%x3	83%(3x3)			21 reps
	2.- C & J	70%(2x3)	75%x3	80%x3	83%(3x3)			21 reps
	3.- Back squat	60%x5	65%x5	70%x5	75%3	80%x3	83%(2x3)	27 reps
	4.- Ab work							
Day 2	1.- Hang Snatch	65%(2x3)	70%x3	75%(3x3)				18 reps
	2.- Jerk b neck	65%(2x3)	70%x3	75%(2x3)				15 reps
	3.- Back squat	60%x5	65%x5	70%x4	75%3	80%(2x3)		23 reps
Day 3	1.- Snatch	65%x3	70%x(2x3)	75%(2x3)				15 reps
	2.- C&J	65%x3	70%x(2x3)	75%(2x3)				15 reps
		65%x5	70%x5	75%x5	80%(2x3)			21 reps
Day 4	1.- Snatch	65%x3	70%x3	75%x2	80%x2	85%x2	90%x2	Max out
		95%x1	100%x1	105%x1				day
	2.- C&J	65%x3	70%x3	75%x2	80%x2	85%x2	90%x2	
		95%x1	100%x1	105%x1				
Obs	210 reps. 71 snatch. 68 C&J. 71 squat						

Week 10	Macrocycle I. Mesocycle III. Microcycle II							
Day 1	1.- Power Snatch	60%(2x4)	65%(3x3)	70%x3	75%(2x3)			26 reps
	2.- P Cl + 3 P J	65%(3x1-1)2	70%(3x1-1)2	75%(3x1-1)3	80%(3x1-)2			27 reps
	3.- Back Squats	60%(2x5)	65%(2x5)	70%(2x5)	75%(2x3)	80%x3	83%(2x3)	45 reps
	4.- Snatch Pull	90%(2x3)	93%(2x3)					12 reps
Day 2	1.- Power Snatch	60%x3	65%(2x3)	70%x3	75%(2x3)			18 reps
	2.- Jerk behind neck	60%x5	70%x5	70%(2x3)	75%(2x3)			20 reps
	3.- Front squats	70%(2x5)	75%(2x5)	80%(2x4)	85%(2x4)			43 reps
Day 3	1.- Power Snatch	60%x4	65%x3	70%(2x3)	75%(2x3)	80%x3		22 reps
	2.- PC + 4PJ	60%(4x1-1)2	65%(4x1-1)2	70%(4x1-1)2				24 reps
	3.- Front squats	65%x5	70%(2x5)	75%(2x4)	80%x4	85%x3	90%(2x3)	37 reps
Day 4	1.- Snatch	60%x3	65%(2x3)	70%x3	75%x3	80%x3	85%x2	25 reps
		87%x1	70%x2	90%(2x1)				
	2.- C&J	60%x3	65%(2x3)	70%x3	75%x3	80%x3	85%x3	25 reps
		87%x2	70%x2	90%(2x1)				
	3.- Back Squats	87%x1	70%x2	90%(2x1)				32 reps
		80%x3	85%x3	90%(2x2)	95%x1	100%x1		
	4.- Snatch Pull	90%(3x3)	93%(2x3)					15 reps
Obs	371 reps. 91 snatch. 96 C&J. 157 squat. 27 pulls.							

Week 11	Macrocycle I. Mesocycle III. Microcycle III									
Day 1	1.- Power Snatch	60%x4	65%(2x3)	70%x3	75%x3	80%x3	83%(2x2)			23 reps
	2.- PCl+3 PJ	65%(3x1-1)	70%(3x1-1)3	75%(3x1-1)	78%(3x1-1)2					24 reps
	3.- Back squat	55%x5	60%x5	65%(2x5)	70%(2x3)	75%x3	80%x3	85%x3		35 reps
	4.- Snatch Pulls	90%(2x3)	93%(2x3)							12 reps
Day 2	1.- Power Snatch	60%x3	65%(2x3)	70%x3	75%(2x3)					18 reps
	2.- Jerk behind neck	65%x5	70%x5	75%(2x3)	78%(2x3)					20 reps
	3.- Front squat	70%x5	75%(2x5)	80%(2x4)	85%x4	90%x2				29 reps
Day 3	1.- Power Snatch	60%x4	65%(2x3)	70%x3	75%x3	80%x3	83%(2x2)			23 reps
	2.- P Cl + fro squ+PJ	60%(4x1-1)2	65%(4x1-1)2	70%94x1-1)2						24 reps
	3.-Front squat	70%x5	75%(2x4)	80%x4	85%x3	90%(2x3)				26 reps
Day 4	1.- Snatch	55%x3	60%x3	65%x3	70%x3	75%x3	80%x2	85%x1	65%x2	22 reps
		92%(2x1)								
	2.- C & J	50%x3	55%(2x3)	60%x3	65%x3	70%x3	75%x2	80%x1	85%x1	24 reps
	3.- Back squats	90%(2x1)								
		45%x5	50%x5	55%x5	60%x4	65%x3	70%x3	75%x3	80%x3	35 reps
		85%x2	90%x2	93%x1	96%x1					
	4.- Snatch Pulls	90%(2x3)	93%(2x3)							12 reps
Obs	327 reps. 86 snatch. 92 C&J. 125 squat. 24 pulls.									

*Clarification Note:

On Day 4, back squats start at 45%X5.

C&J Workout ends at 90%/2x1

Week 12	Macrocycle I. Mesocycle III. Microcycle IV - Competition modeling or control test							
Day 1	1.- Snatch	65%(2x3)	70%x3	75%x3	80%(3x3)			21 reps
	2.- C&J	65%(2x3)	70%x3	75%x3	80%(3x3)			21 reps
	3.- Back Squat	55%x5	60%x5	65%x4	70%x3	75%x3	80%x3	29 reps
		85%x3						
	4.- Snatch pull	90%(2x3)	93%(2x3)					12 reps
Day 2	1.- Hang Snatch	65%x3	70%x3	75%x3	80%(3x3)			18 reps
	2.- Jerk B neck	65%x3	65%x3	70%x3	75%(2x3)			15 reps
	3.- Back Squat	55%x5	60%x5	65%x4	70%x3	75%x3	80%x3	23 reps
Day 3	1.- Snatch	65%(2x3)	70%x3	75%x3	80%(2x3)			18 reps
	2.- C&J	60%(2x3)	65%x3	70%x3	75%x3	77%(2x3)		21 reps
	3.- Back Squat	55%x5	60%x5	65%x4	70%x3	75%x3	80%x3	29 reps
		85%(2x3)						
Day 4	1.- Snatch	65%x3	70%(2x3)	75%x3	80%x2	85%x1	90%x1	21 reps
		95%x1	70%x2	100%x1	105%x1			
	2.- C&J	65%x3	70%(2x3)	75%x3	80%x2	85%x1	90%x1	21 reps
		95%x1	70%x2	100%x1	105%x1			
Obs	249 reps. 78 snatch, 78 C&J. 81 squat.12 pulls							

Gwendolyn Sisto and Ivan Rojas

5 days a week program

Week 1	Macrocycle I, Mesocycle I, Microcycle I						
Day 1	1.-Power Snatch	60%(2x3)	65%(2x3)	70%(2x3)			18 reps
	2.-P. Clean & P. Jerk	65%(3x1-2)	70%(3x1-2)	75%(3x1-2)			18 reps
	3.-Back Squat	60%(2x4)	65%(2x4)	70%x3	75%x3	80%(2x3)	28 reps
	4.-Snatch Pull	80%(2x3)	85%(2x3)				12 reps
	5.-Ab work						
	6.-Light jogg	15 minutes					
Day 2	1.-Power Snatch	60%(2x3)	65%(2x3)	70%(2x3)			18 reps
	2.-P. Clean & P. Jerk	65%(3x1-2)	70%(3x1-2)	75%(3x1-2)			18 reps
	3.-Back Squat	60%(2x4)	65%x4	70%x3	75%(2x3)	80%(2x3)	27 reps
	4.-Snatch Pull	80%(2x3)	85%(2x3)				12 reps
	5.-Ab work						
	6.-Light jogg	15 minutes					
Day 3	1.- Snatch	70%x3	75%(2x3)	80%x3	83%x3		15 reps
	2.- C & J	65%x3	70%x3	75%(2x3)	80%x3		15 reps
	3.- Front Squat	65%x5	70%(2x4)	80%(2x4)			24 reps
		Ab work					
Day 4	1.-Power Snatch	60%(2x3)	65%x3	70%x3	73%x3		15 reps
	2.- Jerk behind neck	65%(2x3)	70%(2x3)	75%(2x3)			18 reps
	3.- Front Squat	65%x5	70%x4	75%x4	80%(2x3)		19 reps
	4.-Snatch Pull	80%(2x3)	85%(2x3)				12 reps
	5.-Ab work						
Day 5	1.- Snatch	60%x3	65%(2x3)	70%x3	75%(2x3)	80%(2x3)	24 reps
	2.- C & J	60%x3	65%(2x3)	70%x3	75%(2x3)	80%(2x3)	24 reps
	3.-Back Squat	60%(2x4)	65%x4	70%x3	75%(2x3)	80%(2x3)	85%(2x2)	31 reps
	4.-Snatch Pull	85%(2x2)					31 reps
	5.-Ab work	80%(2x3)	85%(2x3)				12 reps
Obs	360 reps. 90 snatches, 93 C&J, 129 squats, 48 pulls.						

Week 2	Macrocycle I, Mesocycle I, Microcycle II						
Day 1	1.- Power Snatch	60%(2x3)	65%(2x3)	70%x3	75%x3		15 reps
	2.- P. Clean+ 3 PJ	65%(3x1-1)	70%(3x1-1)	75%(3x1-1)	80%(3x1-2)		15 reps
	3.- Back Squat	60%(2x5)	65%(2x5)	70%x4	75%x3	80%(2x3)	35 reps
	4.- Snatch pull	85%(2x3)	90%(2x3)				12 reps
	5.- Ab work						
	6.- Light jogg	15 minutes					
Day 2	1.- P. Sn Bel Knee	60%(2x3)	65%(2x3)	70%x3	75%x3		15 reps
	2.- P. Clean+ 3 PJ	65%(3x1-1)	70%(3x1-1)	75%(3x1-1)	80%(3x1-2)		15 reps
	3.- Back Squat	60%(2x4)	65%x4	70%x3	75%(2x3)	80%3	85%(2x3)	27 reps
	4.- Snatch pull	85%(2x3)	90%(2x3)				12 reps
	5.- Ab work						
Day 3	1.- Snatch	60%x3	65%x3	70%x3	75%x3	80%x3	15 reps
	2.- C & J	60%x3	65%x3	70%x3	75%x3	80%x3	15 reps
	3.- Back Squat	70%(2x4)	75%(2x4)	80%x4	85%(2x3)		26 reps
	4.- Snatch pull	85%(2x3)	90%(2x3)				12 reps
	5.- Ab work						
Day 4	1.- Power Snatch	60%x3	65%x3	70%x3	73%(2x3)		15 reps
	2.- Jerk Behind neck	65%(2x3)	70%(2x3)	75%x3	805x3		18 reps
	3.- Front Squat	65%x5	70%x5	75%x5	80%x4		23 reps
	4.- Ab work						
Day 5	1.- Snatch	60%x3	65%(2x3)	70%x3	75%x3	80%x3	85%x2	20 reps
	2.- C & J	55%x3	60%x3	65%x3	70%x3	75%x3	80%x3	
		85%x2					20 reps
	3.- Back Squat	55%x5	60%x5	65%x5	70%x5	75%x4	80%x5	
		85%x3	90%(2x2)				36 reps
	346 reps. 80 snatches. 83 C&J. 147 squats. 36 pulls.						

Week 3	Macrocycle I, Mesocycle I, Microcycle III							
Day 1	1.- Power Snatch	60%(2x3)	65% x 3	70%x3	75%x3	80%(2x3)		21 reps
	2.- P Clean+P Jerk	65%(3x1-1)2	70%(3x1-1)	75%(3x1-1)2	80%(3x1-1)2			21 reps
	3.- Back Squat	60%(3x5)	65%(2x5)	70%x4	75%x3	80%(2x3)		38 reps
	4.- Snatch Pull	85%(2x3)	90%(2x3)					12 reps
Day 2	1.- Snatch	65%x3	70%x3	75%x3	80%x3	85%x3	90%x2	17 reps
	2.- C & J	65%x3	70%x3	75%x3	80%x3	85%x3	90%x2	17 reps
	3.- Front Squat	70%(2x4)	75%(2x4)	80%x4	85%(2x3)			26 reps
	4.- Snatch Pull	85%(2x3)	90%(2x3)					12 reps
	5.- Ab work							
Day 3	1.- P Snatch below kn	50%(2x3)	55%(2x3)	60%x3	70%x3	75%(2x3)		21 reps
	2.- P Clean+P Jerk	65%(3x1-1)2	70%(3x1-1)	75%(3x1-1)2	80%(3x1-1)2			21 reps
	3.- Back Squat	60%(2x5)	65%(2x5)	70%x4	75%x3	80%x3	85%x3	33 reps
	4.- Snatch Pull	85%(2x3)	90%(2x3)					12 reps
Day 4	1.- P Snatch	60%x3	65%x3	70%x3	75%(2x3)			15 reps
	2.- Jerk Behind Neck	65%(2x3)	70%(2x3)	75%(2x3)	80%x3			21 reps
	3.- Front Squat	65%(2x5)	70%x5	75%x5	80%(2x5)			30 reps
Day 5	1.- Snatch	65%x3	70%(2x3)	75%x3	80%x3	85%x3	90%x2	25 reps
		80%x3	90%x2					
	2.- C & J	55%x3	60%x3	65%x3	70%x3	75% x3	80%x3	25 reps
		85%x3	80%x2	90%x2				
	3.- Back Squat	50%x5	55%x4	60%x4	65%x4	70%(2x3)	75%x3	36 reps
		80%(2x3)	85%x2	90%x2				
	4.- Snatch Pull	85%(2x3)	90%(2x3)					12 reps
Obs	415 reps. 99 snatch. 105 C&J. 163 squats. 48 pulls.							

Week 4	Macrocycle I. Mesocycle I. Microcycle 3								
Day 1	1.- Power Snatch	65%x3	70%(2x3)	75%x3	80%x3	83%x3			18 reps
	2.- P Clean + 3 P Jerks	65%(3x1-1)	70%(3x1-1)	75%(3x1-2)	80%(3x1-1)	83%(3x1-1)			18 reps
	3.- Back Squat	60%x5	65%(2x5)	70%x5	75%x3	80%x3	83%x3		29 reps
	4.- Snatch Pulls	85%(2x3)	90%(2x3)						12 reps
Day 2	1.- P Snatch Below Knees	65%x3	70%(2x3)	75%x3	80%x3	83%x3			18 reps
	2.- Jerk behind neck	70%x4	75%x3	80%(3x3)					20 reps
	3.- Back Squat	60%x4	65%(2x4)	70%x3	75%x3	80%x3	83%(2x3)		27 reps
	4.- Snatch Pulls	85%(2x3)	90%(2x3)						12 reps
	5.- Ab work								
Day 3	1.- Snatch	65%x3	70%x3	75%x3	80%x3	83%x3			15 reps
	2.- C & J	65%x3	70%x3	75%x3	80%x3	85%x3			15 reps
	3.- Fron Squat	70%(2x5)	75%(2x5)	80%x4	85%(2x3)				30 reps
	4.- Ab work								
Day 4	1.- Power Snatch	60%x3	65%x3	70%x3	75%(2x3)				15 reps
	2.- Jerk behind neck	65%(2x3)	70%(2x3)	75%x3	80%x3				18 reps
	3.- Front Squat	65%x5	70%x5	75%x5	80%(2x5)				25 reps
	4.- Ab work								
Day 5	1.- Snatch	65%x3	70%(2x3)	75%x3	80%x3	85%x3	90%x1	92%x1	20 reps
	2.- C & J	60%x3	65%(2x3)	70%x3	75%x3	80%x3	85%x2	90%x1	
		92%x1							22 reps
	3.- Back Squat	60%x4	65%x4	70%x4	75%x4	80%x3	85%x3	90%x3	
		92%x1	95%x1						29 reps
	4.- Snatch Pulls	85%(2x3)	90%(2x3)						12 reps
Obser	355 reps. 86 snatch. 93 C&J. 140 squats. 36 pulls.								

Week 5	Macrocycle I, Mesocycle II, Microcycle I							
Day 1	1.- Power Snatch	60%(2x3)	65%x3	70%x3	75%x3	80%(2x3)		21 reps
	2.- P C +3P Jerks	65%(3x1-2)	70%(3x1-1)	75%(3x1-2)	80%(3x1-2)			21 reps
	3.- Back Squats	60%(3x5)	65%(2x5)	70%x4	75%x3	80%x3	83%x3	38 reps
	4.- Snatch Pull	85%(2x3)	90%(2x3)					12 reps
	5.- Ab work							
Day 2	1.- P Snatch bel kn	60%(2x3)	65%x3	70%x3	75%x3	80%(2x3)		21 reps
	2.- Jerk Behind N	65%x4	70%x4	75%x4	80%(3x3)			21 reps
	3.- Back Squats	60%x5	65%(2x5)	70%x3	75%x3	80%(2x3)	85%(2x3)	33 reps
	4.- SnatchPull	85%(2x3)	90%(2x3)					12 reps
	5.- Ab work							
Day 3	1.- Snatch	65%x3	70%x3	75%x3	80%x3	85%x3	90%x2	17 reps
	2.- C & J	65%x3	70%x3	75%x3	80%x3	85%x3	90%(2x2)	19 reps
	3.- Front Squat	70%(2x4)	75%(2x4)	80%x4	85%(2x3)			26 reps
	4.- Ab work							
Day 4	1.- Power Snatch	60%(2x3)	65%x3	70%x3	75%x3	80%(2x3)		21 reps
	2.- P C +3P Jerks	65%(3x1-2)	70%(3x1-1)	75%(3x1-2)	80%(3x1-2)			21 reps
	3.- Back Squats	60%x5	65%(2x5)	70%x3	75%x3	80%(2x3)	85%(2x3)	33 reps
Day 5	1.- Snatch	60%x3	65%(2x3)	70%x3	75%x3	80%x3	87%x1	21 reps
		95%(2x1)						
	2.- C & J	60%x3	65%(2x3)	70%x3	75%x3	80%(2x3)	87%x1	24 reps
		95%(2x1)						
	3.- Back Squats	60%(3x5)	65%(2x5)	70%x3	75%x2	80%x2	85%x2	36 reps
		90%x1	95%(2x1)					
	4.- SnatchPull	85%(2x3)	90%(2x3)					12 reps
Obs	409 reps. 101 snatch. 106 C&J. 166 squats. 36 pulls.							

Week 6	Macrocycle I. Mesocycle II. Microcycle II						
Day 1	1.- Power Snatch	70%(2x3)	75%x3	80%x3	83%(2x3)		18 reps
	2.- P Clean +3 PJ	60%(3x1-1)	65%(3x1-1)	70%(3x1-1)	80%(3x1-1)		18 reps
	3.- Back Squat	60%x5	65%x5	70%x5	75%x3	80%x3	27 reps
		83%(3x2)					
	4.- Snatch pull	85%(2x3)	90%(2x3)				12 reps
Day 2	1.- P Snatch B Kn	70%(2x3)	75%x3	80%x3	83%(2x3)		18 reps
	2.- Jerk b neck	60%x4	65%x4	70%x4	75%x3	80%(2x3)	21 reps
	3.- Front squat	70%(2x5)	75%(2x5)	80%x4	85%x3	87%x3	30 reps
	4.- Snatch pull	85%(2x3)	90%(2x3)				12 reps
Day 3	1.- Snatch	70%(2x3)	75%x3	80%x3	83%x3		15 reps
	2.- C & J	70%(2x3)	75%x3	80%x3	83%x3		15 reps
	3.- Back Squat	60%x5	65%x5	70%x5	75%(2x3)	80%(2x3)	27 reps
	4.- Snatch pull	85%(2x3)	90%(2x3)				12 reps
Day 4	1.- Power Snatch	70%(2x3)	75%x3	80%x3	83%x3		15 reps
	2.- 1 PC + 3 PJ	60%(3x1-2)	65%(3x1-1)	70%(3x1-1)			15 reps
	3.- Front squat	65%x5	70%x5	75%x5	80%(2x5)		25 reps
	4.- Snatch w bar	5x3					
	5.- C&J w bar	5x3					
Day 5	1.- Snatch	65%x3	70%(2x3)	75%x3	80%x3	85%x2	21 reps
		90%x2	95%(2x1)				
	2.- C & J	65%x3	70%(2x3)	75%x3	80%x2	85%x2	23 reps
		90%x2	95%x1	97%x1			
	3.- Back Squat	50%x4	55%x4	60%x4	65%x4	70%x3	30 reps
		75%x3	80%x3	85%x2	90%x1	95%x1	
		100%x1					
	4.- Snatch pull	85%(2x3)	90%(2x3)				12 reps
Obs	354 reps. 87 snatch. 92 C&J.139 squats. 36 pulls.						

Week 7	Macrocycle I, Mesocycle II, Microcycle III						
Day 1	1.-Hang Snatch	60%(2x3)	65%x3	70%x3	75%(3x3)			21 reps
	2.- p Cl + 3 PJ	55%(3x1-1)	60%(3x1-1)	65%(3x1-1)	70%(3x1-1)	75%(3x1-1)	80%(3x1-1)	19 reps
		85%(3x1-2)						
	3.- Back squat	60%x5	65%x5	70%x5	75%x4	80%x4	83%(2x3)	29 reps
	4.- Santch Pulls	90%(2x3)	95%(2x3)					12 reps
Day 2	1.- Snatch	65%(2x3)	70%x3	75%x3	87%x3	85%(2x3)		21 reps
	2.- C&J	65%(2x3)	70%x3	75%x3	87%x3	85%(2x3)		21 reps
	3.- Front Squat	70%x5	75%x5	80%x4	85%x2	87%x2	90%x2	22 reps
		95%x2						
	4.- Santch Pulls	90%(2x3)	95%(2x3)					12 reps
Day 3	1.- Snatch	70%2x3	75%x3	80%x3	83%x3			15 reps
	2.- C&J	70%2x3	75%x3	80%x3	83%x3			15 reps
	3.- Back squat	60%x5	65%(2x5)	70%x3	75%x3	80%(2x3)		27 reps
Day 4	1.- P. Snatch	70%2x3	75%x3	80%x3	83%x3			15 reps
	2.- Jerk bn	70%2x3	75%(2x3)	80%x3	83%x3			18 reps
	3.- Front Squat	65%x5	70%x5	75%x4	80%(2x3)	85%(2x2)		24 reps
	4.- Snatch Bar	3X5						
	5.- C&J Bar	3X5						
Day 5	1.- Snatch	65%x3	70%x3	75%x3	87%x3	85%x2	90%1	17 reps
		95%x1	100%x1					
	2.- C&J	65%x3	70%x3	75%x3	87%x3	85%x2	90%1	17 reps
		95%x1	100%x1					
Obs	305 reps. 89 snatch. 90 C&J. 102 squat. 24 pulls						

Week 8	Macrocycle I, Mesocycle II, Microcycle IV							
Day 1	1.-Power Snatch	70%(2x3)	75%x3	80%x3	83%(3x3)				21 reps
	2.-P Clean+3PJ	60%(3x1-1)	65%(3x1-2)	70%(3x1-1)	75%(3x1-1)	80%(3x1-2)		21 reps
	3.-Back Squat	60%x5	65%x5	70%x5	75%x3	80%x3	85%x3	87%(2x3)	30 reps
	4.- Snatch pull	90%(2x3)	95%(3x3)						12 reps
Day 2	1.- Snatch	70%(2x3)	75%x3	80%x3	83%x3	85%(2x3)		21 reps
	2.- C&J	75%(2x3)	70%(2x3)	80%x3	80%x3	85%x3	87%x3	21 reps
	3.- Front Squat	70%x5	75%(2x5)	80%x4	85%(2x3)	87%x3	90%x2	30 reps
	4.- Snatch pull	90%(2x3)	95%(2x3)						12 reps
Day 3	1.- Hang P. Snatch	65%(2x3)	70%x3	75%x3	80%(2x3)			15 reps
	2.- J behind neck	70%x3	75%x3	80%x3	85%x3	87%x3		15 reps
	3.- Back Squat	60%x5	65%x5	70%x3	75%x3	80%(2x3)		22 reps
Day 4	1.-P Snatch	70%(2x3)	75%x3	80%(2x3)	83% x3			18 reps
	2.-P Clean+3PJ	60%(3x1-1)	65%(3x1-1)	70%(3x1-1)	75%(3x1-1)	80%(3x1-1)	85%(3x1-2)	21 reps
	3.- Front Squat	65%x5	70%x5	75%x5	80%(2x5)			25 reps
Day 5	1.- Snatch	65%x3	70%(2x3)	75%x3	80%x3	85%x2	90%x2	95%x1	20 reps
	2.- C & J	50%x3	55%(2x3)	60%x3	65%x3	70%x2	75%x2	80%x2	24 reps
		85%x1	90%x1	95%x1	100%x1			
	3.- Back Squat	50%x4	55%x4	60%x4	65%x4	70%x3	75%x3	80%x3	31 reps
		85%x2	90%x2	95%x1	100%x1			
	4.- Snatch pull	90%(2x3)	95%(2x3)						12 reps
Obs	371 reps. 95 snatch. 102 C&J.138 squats. 36 pulls.							

Week 9	Macrocycle I, Mesocycle III, Microcycle I						
Day 1	1.- Snatch	70%(2x3)	75%x3	80%x3	83%(3x3)			21 reps
	2.- C & J	70%(2x3)	75%x3	80%x3	83%(3x3)			21 reps
	3.- Back squat	60%x5	65%x5	70%x5	75%3	80%x3	83%(2x3)	27 reps
	4.- Ab work							
Day 2	1.- Snatch	65%(2x3)	70%(2x3)	75%(3x3)				21 reps
	2.- C & J	65%(2x3)	70%(2x3)	75%(3x3)				21 reps
	3.- Front squat	60%x5	65%x5	70%x5	75%(2x3)	80%x3	83%(2x3)	30 reps
	4.- Ab work							
Day 3	1.- Hang Snatch	65%(2x3)	70%x3	75%(3x3)				18 reps
	2.- Jerk b neck	65%(2x3)	70%x3	75%(2x3)				15 reps
	3.- Back squat	60%x5	65%x5	70%x4	75%3	80%(2x3)		23 reps
Day 4	1.- Snatch	65%x3	70%x(2x3)	75%(2x3)				15 reps
	2.- C&J	65%x3	70%x(2x3)	75%(2x3)				15 reps
		65%x5	70%x5	75%x5	80%(2x3)			21 reps
Day 5	1.- Snatch	65%x3	70%x3	75%x2	80%x2	85%x2	90%x2	Max out
		95%x1	100%x1	105%x1				day
	2.- C&J	65%x3	70%x3	75%x2	80%x2	85%x2	90%x2	
		95%x1	100%x1	105%x1				
	282 reps. 92 snatch. 89 C&J.101 squats.							

Week 10	Macrocycle I. Mesocycle III. Microcycle II						
Day 1	1.- Power Snatch	60%(2x4)	65%(3x3)	70%x3	75%(2x3)			26 reps
	2.- P Cl + 3 P J	65%(3x1-1)2	70%(3x1-1)2	75%(3x1-1)3	80%(3x1-)2			27 reps
	3.- Back Squats	60%(2x5)	65%(2x5)	70%(2x5)	75%(2x3)	80%x3	83%(2x3)	45 reps
	4.- Snatch Pull	90%(2x3)	93%(2x3)					12 reps
Day 2	1.- P Snatch b knee	60%(2x4)	65%(2x3)	70%x3	75%(2x3)			26 reps
	2.- Jerk behind neck	65%(2x3)	70%(2x3)	75%(2x3)	80%(2x3)			24 reps
	3.- Back Squats	60%(2x5)	65%(2x5)	70%(2x5)	75%x4	80%x3	83%(2x3)	43 reps
	4.- Snatch Pull	90%(2x3)	93%(2x3)					12 reps
Day 3	1.- Power Snatch	60%x3	65%(2x3)	70%x3	75%(2x3)			18 reps
	2.- Jerk behind neck	60%x5	70%x5	70%(2x3)	75%(2x3)			20 reps
	3.- Front squats	70%(2x5)	75%(2x5)	80%(2x4)	85%(2x4)			43 reps
Day 4	1.- Power Snatch	60%x4	65%x3	70%(2x3)	75%(2x3)	80%x3		22 reps
	2.- PC + 4PJ	60%(4x1-1)2	65%(4x1-1)2	70%(4x1-1)2				24 reps
	3.- Front squats	65%x5	70%(2x5)	75%(2x4)	80%x4	85%x3	90%(2x3)	12 reps
Day 5	1.- Snatch	60%x3	65%(2x3)	70%x3	75%x3	80%x3	85%x2	25 reps
		87%x1	70%x2	90%(2x1)				
	2.- C&J	60%x3	65%(2x3)	70%x3	75%x3	80%x3	85%x3	25 reps
		87%x2	70%x2	90%(2x1)				
	3.- Back Squats	87%x1	70%x2	90%(2x1)				32 reps
		80%x3	85%x3	90%(2x2)	95%x1	100%x1		
	4.- Snatch Pull	90%(3x3)	93%(2x3)					15 reps
Obs	475 reps. 117 snatch. 120 C&J. 187 Squats. 51 pulls.						

Week 11	Macrocycle I. Mesocycle III. Microcycle III								
Day 1	1.- Power Snatch	60%x4	65%(2x3)	70%x3	75%x3	80%x3	83%(2x2)			23 reps
	2.- PCl+3 PJ	65%(3x1-1)	70%(3x1-1)3	75%(3x1-1)	78%(3x1-1)2					24 reps
	3.- Back squat	55%x5	60%x5	65%(2x5)	70%(2x3)	75%x3	80%x3	85%x3		35 reps
	4.- Snatch Pulls	90%(2x3)	93%(2x3)							12 reps
Day 2	1.- P Snatch b knee	60%x4	65%x3	70%(2x3)	75%x3	80%x3				19 reps
	2.- Back squat + Jerk	45%(2x3)	50%(2x3)	55%(2x3)	60%(2x3)					24 reps
	3.- Back squats	60%x5	65%x5	70%(2x3)	75%x3	80%x3	85%(2x3)			28 reps
	4.- Snatch Pulls	90%(2x3)	93%(2x3)							12 reps
Day 3	1.- Power Snatch	60%x3	65%(2x3)	70%x3	75%(2x3)					18 reps
	2.- Jerk behind neck	65%x5	70%x5	75%(2x3)	78%(2x3)					20 reps
	3.- Front squat	70%x5	75%(2x5)	80%(2x4)	85%x4	90%x2				29 reps
Day 4	1.- Power Snatch	60%x4	65%(2x3)	70%x3	75%x3	80%x3	83%(2x2)			23 reps
	2.- P Cl + fro squ+PJ	60%(4x1-1)2	65%(4x1-1)2	70%94x1-1)2						24 reps
	3.-Front squat	70%x5	75%(2x4)	80%x4	85%x3	90%(2x3)				26 reps
Day 5	1.- Snatch	55%x3	60%x3	65%x3	70%x3	75%x3	80%x2	85%x1	65%x2	22 reps
		92%(2x1)								
	2.- C & J	50%x3	55%(2x3)	60%x3	65%x3	70%x3	75%x2	80%x1	85%x1	24 reps
	3.- Back squats	90%(2x1)								
		45%x5	50%x5	55%x5	60%x4	65%x3	70%x3	75%x3	80%x3	35 reps
		85%x2	90%x2	93%x1	96%x1					
	4.- Snatch Pulls	90%(2x3)	93%(2x3)							12 reps
Obs	410 reps. 105 snatch. 116 C&J. 153 squats. 36 pulls.								

*Clarification Note:

On Day 4, back squats start at 45%X5.

C&J Workout ends at 90%/2x1

Week 12	Macrocycle I. Mesocycle III. Microcycle IV - Competition modeling or control test							
Day 1	1.- Snatch	65%(2x3)	70%x3	75%x3	80%(3x3)			21 reps
	2.- C&J	65%(2x3)	70%x3	75%x3	80%(3x3)			21 reps
	3.- Back Squat	55%x5	60%x5	65%x4	70%x3	75%x3	80%x3	29 reps
		85%x3						
	4.- Snatch pull	90%(2x3)	93%(2x3)					12 reps
Day 2	1.- Snatch	65%(2x3)	70%(2x3)	75%(3x3)				21 reps
	2.- C&J	65%(2x3)	70%(2x3)	75%(3x3)				21 reps
	3.- Front Squat	70%x5	75%(2x5)	80%x4	85%(2x3)	87%x3	90%(2x1)	30 reps
Day 3	1.- Hang Snatch	65%x3	70%x3	75%x3	80%(3x3)			18 reps
	2.- Jerk B neck	65%x3	65%x3	70%x3	75%(2x3)			15 reps
	3.- Back Squat	55%x5	60%x5	65%x4	70%x3	75%x3	80%x3	23 reps
Day 4	1.- Snatch	65%(2x3)	70%x3	75%x3	80%(2x3)			18 reps
	2.- C&J	60%(2x3)	65%x3	70%x3	75%x3	77%(2x3)		21 reps
	3.- Back Squat	55%x5	60%x5	65%x4	70%x3	75%x3	80%x3	29 reps
		85%(2x3)						
Day 5	1.- Snatch	65%x3	70%(2x3)	75%x3	80%x2	85%x1	90%x1	22 reps
		95%x1	70%x2	100%x1	105%x1			
	2.- C&J	65%x3	70%(2x3)	75%x3	80%x2	85%x1	90%x1	21 reps
		95%x1	70%x2	100%x1	105%x1			
Obs	322 reps. 100 snatch. 99 C&J.111 Squats. 12 pulls.							

Gwendolyn Sisto and Ivan Rojas

6 days a week program

Week 1	Macrocycle I, Mesocycle I, Microcycle I						
Day 1	1.-Power Snatch	60%(2x3)	65%(2x3)	70%(2x3)			18 reps
	2.-P. Clean & P. Jerk	65%(3x1-2)	70%(3x1-2)	75%(3x1-2)			18 reps
	3.-Back Squat	60%(2x4)	65%(2x4)	70%x3	75%x3	80%(2x3)	28 reps
	4.-Snatch Pull	80%(2x3)	85%(2x3)				12 reps
Day 2	1.-Power Snatch	60%(2x3)	65%(2x3)	70%(2x3)			18 reps
	2.-P. Clean & P. Jerk	65%(3x1-2)	70%(3x1-2)	75%(3x1-2)			18 reps
	3.-Back Squat	60%(2x4)	65%x4	70%x3	75%(2x3)	80%(2x3)	27 reps
	4.-Snatch Pull	80%(2x3)	85%(2x3)				12 reps
Day 3	1.- Snatch	70%x3	75%(2x3)	80%x3	83%x3		15 reps
	2.- C & J	65%x3	70%x3	75%(2x3)	80%x3		15 reps
	3.- Front Squat	65%x5	70%(2x4)	80%(2x4)			24 reps
Day 4	1.-Power Snatch	60%(2x3)	65%x3	70%x3	73%x3		15 reps
	2.- Jerk behind neck	65%(2x3)	70%(2x3)	75%(2x3)			18 reps
	3.- Front Squat	65%x5	70%x4	75%x4	80%(2x3)		19 reps
	4.-Snatch Pull	80%(2x3)	85%(2x3)				12 reps
	5.-Ab work						
Day 5	1.- Snatch	60%x3	65%(2x3)	70%x3	75%(2x3)		18 reps
	2.- C & J	65%(2x3)	70%x3	75%(2x3)			18 reps
	3.-Back Squat	55%x5	60%x5	65%x5	70%x4	75%x4	80%(2x3)	29 reps
	4.-Snatch Pull	80%(2x3)	85%(2x3)				12 reps
	5.-Ab work						
Day 6	1.- Snatch	60%x3	65%(2x3)	70%x3	75%(2x3)	80%(2x3)	24 reps
	2.- C & J	60%x3	65%(2x3)	70%x3	75%(2x3)	80%(2x3)	24 reps
	3.-Back Squat	60%(2x4)	65%x4	70%x3	75%(2x3)	80%(2x3)	85%(2x2)	31 reps
	4.-Snatch Pull	85%(2x2)					31 reps
	5.-Ab work	80%(2x3)	85%(2x3)				12 reps
Obs	Microcycle of introduction to prepare the organism.437 reps, snatch 108, C&J 111, squats 158, pulls 60						

Week 2	Macrocycle I, Mesocycle I, Microcycle II						
Day 1	1.- Power Snatch	60%(2x3)	65%(2x3)	70%x3	75%x3			15 reps
	2.- P. Clean+ 3 PJ	65%(3x1-1)	70%(3x1-1)	75%(3x1-1)	80%(3x1-2)			15 reps
	3.- Back Squat	60%(2x5)	65%(2x5)	70%x4	75%x3	80%(2x3)		35 reps
	4.- Snatch pull	85%(2x3)	90%(2x3)					12 reps
Day 2	1.- P. Sn Bel Knee	60%(2x3)	65%(2x3)	70%x3	75%x3			15 reps
	2.- P. Clean+ 3 PJ	65%(3x1-1)	70%(3x1-1)	75%(3x1-1)	80%(3x1-2)			15 reps
	3.- Back Squat	60%(2x4)	65%x4	70%x3	75%(2x3)	80%3	85%(2x3)	27 reps
	4.- Snatch pull	85%(2x3)	90%(2x3)					12 reps
Day 3	1.- Snatch	60%x3	65%x3	70%x3	75%x3	80%x3		15 reps
	2.- C & J	60%x3	65%x3	70%x3	75%x3	80%x3		15 reps
	3.- Back Squat	70%(2x4)	75%(2x4)	80%x4	85%(2x3)			26 reps
	4.- Snatch pull	85%(2x3)	90%(2x3)					12 reps
Day 4	1.- Power Snatch	60%x3	65%x3	70%x3	73%(2x3)			15 reps
	2.- Jerk Behind neck	65%(2x3)	70%(2x3)	75%x3	805x3			18 reps
	3.- Front Squat	65%x5	70%x5	75%x5	80%x4			23 reps
	4.- Ab work							
Day 5	1.- Snatch	60%x3	65%(2x3)	70%x3	75%x3	80%x3		18 reps
	2.- C & J	55%x3	60%(2x3)	65%x3	70%x3	75%x3		18 reps
	3.- Back Squat	55%x5	60%x5	65%x5	70%x4	75%x3	80%x5	30 reps
		85%x3						
	4.- Snatch pull	85%(3x3)	90%(2x3)					12 reps
Day 6	1.- Snatch	60%x3	65%(2x3)	70%x3	75%x3	80%x3	85%x2	20 reps
	2.- C & J	55%x3	60%x3	65%x3	70%x3	75%x3	80%x3	
		85%x2						20 reps
	3.- Back Squat	55%x5	60%x5	65%x5	70%x5	75%x4	80%x5	30 reps
	4.- Snatch pull	85%x3	90%(2x2)					36 reps
	Microcycle of special preparation unloading. 370 reps. Snatch 85. C&J 91. Squats 343. Pulls 51							

Week 3	Macrocycle I, Mesocycle I, Microcycle III							
Day 1	1.- Power Snatch	60%(2x3)	65% x 3	70%x3	75%x3	80%(2x3)		21 reps
	2.- P Clean+P Jerk	65%(3x1-1)2	70%(3x1-1)	75%(3x1-1)2	80%(3x1-1)2			21 reps
	3.- Back Squat	60%(3x5)	65%(2x5)	70%x4	75%x3	80%(2x3)		38 reps
	4.- Snatch Pull	85%(2x3)	90%(2x3)					12 reps
Day 2	1.- Snatch	65%x3	70%x3	75%x3	80%x3	85%x3	90%x2	17 reps
	2.- C & J	65%x3	70%x3	75%x3	80%x3	85%x3	90%x2	17 reps
	3.- Front Squat	70%(2x4)	75%(2x4)	80%x4	85%(2x3)			26 reps
	4.- Snatch Pull	85%(2x3)	90%(2x3)					12 reps
	5.- Ab work							
Day 3	1.- P Snatch below kn	50%(2x3)	55%(2x3)	60%x3	70%x3	75%(2x3)		21 reps
	2.- P Clean+P Jerk	65%(3x1-1)2	70%(3x1-1)	75%(3x1-1)2	80%(3x1-1)2			21 reps
	3.- Back Squat	60%(2x5)	65%(2x5)	70%x4	75%x3	80%x3	85%x3	33 reps
	4.- Snatch Pull	85%(2x3)	90%(2x3)					12 reps
Day 4	1.- P Snatch	60%x3	65%x3	70%x3	75%(2x3)			15 reps
	2.- Jerk Behind Neck	65%(2x3)	70%(2x3)	75%(2x3)	80%x3			21 reps
	3.- Front Squat	65%(2x5)	70%x5	75%x5	80%(2x5)			30 reps
Day 5	1.- Snatch	60%(2x3)	65% x 3	70%x3	75%(2x3)	80%x3		21 reps
	2.- C & J	55%x3	60%(2x3)	65%x3	70%(2x3)	75%x3		21 reps
	3.- Back Squat	55%x5	60%x5	65%x5	70%x5	75%x4	80%x4	31 reps
		85%x3						
	4.- Snatch Pull	85%(2x3)	90%(2x3)					12 reps
Day 6	1.- Snatch	65%x3	70%(2x3)	75%x3	80%x3	85%x3	90%x2	25 reps
		80%x3	90%x2					
	2.- C & J	55%x3	60%x3	65%x3	70%x3	75% x3	80%x3	25 reps
		85%x3	80%x2	90%x2				
	3.- Back Squat	50%x5	55%x4	60%x4	65%x4	70%(2x3)	75%x3	36 reps
		80%(2x3)	85%x2	90%x2				
	4.- Snatch Pull	85%(2x3)	90%(2x3)					12 reps
Obs	Macrocycle of preparation. High volume medium intensity. 508 rps. Snatch 120 reps, C&J 126, Squats 194							
	pulls 68							

Week 4	Macrocycle I. Mesocycle I. Microcycle 3								
Day 1	1.- Power Snatch	65%x3	70%(2x3)	75%x3	80%x3	83%x3			18 reps
	2.- P Clean + 3 P Jerks	65%(3x1-1)	70%(3x1-1)	75%(3x1-2)	80%(3x1-1)	83%(3x1-1)			18 reps
	3.- Back Squat	60%x5	65%(2x5)	70%x5	75%x3	80%x3	83%x3		29 reps
	4.- Snatch Pulls	85%(2x3)	90%(2x3)						12 reps
Day 2	1.- P Snatch Below Knees	65%x3	70%(2x3)	75%x3	80%x3	83%x3			18 reps
	2.- Jerk behind neck	70%x4	75%x3	80%(3x3)					20 reps
	3.- Back Squat	60%x4	65%(2x4)	70%x3	75%x3	80%x3	83%(2x3)		27 reps
	4.- Snatch Pulls	85%(2x3)	90%(2x3)						12 reps
Day 3	1.- Snatch	65%x3	70%x3	75%x3	80%x3	83%x3			15 reps
	2.- C & J	65%x3	70%x3	75%x3	80%x3	85%x3			15 reps
	3.- Fron Squat	70%(2x5)	75%(2x5)	80%x4	85%(2x3)				30 reps
Day 4	1.- Power Snatch	60%x3	65%x3	70%x3	75%(2x3)				15 reps
	2.- Jerk behind neck	65%(2x3)	70%(2x3)	75%x3	80%x3				18 reps
	3.- Front Squat	65%x5	70%x5	75%x5	80%(2x5)				25 reps
Day 5	1.- Snatch	65%x3	70%(2x3)	75%x3	80%x3	83%x3			18 reps
	2.- C & J	60%x3	65%(2x3)	70%x3	75%x3	80%x3			18 reps
	3.- Back Squat	55%x5	60%x5	65%x5	70%x4	75%x3	80%x3	83%x3	28 reps
	4.- Snatch Pulls	85%(2x3)	90%(2x3)						12 reps
Day 6	1.- Snatch	65%x3	70%(2x3)	75%x3	80%x3	85%x3	90%x1	92%x1	20 reps
	2.- C & J	60%x3	65%(2x3)	70%x3	75%x3	80%x3	85%x2	90%x1	
		92%x1							22 reps
	3.- Back Squat	60%x4	65%x4	70%x4	75%x4	80%x3	85%x3	90%x3	
		92%x1	95%x1						29 reps
	4.- Snatch Pulls	85%(2x3)	90%(2x3)						12 reps
Obser	Microcycle of unloading. Reps 431. Snatch 104. C&J 111. Squats 168. Pulls 48.								

Week 5	Macrocycle I, Mesocycle II, Microcycle I							
Day 1	1.- Power Snatch	60%(2x3)	65%x3	70%x3	75%x3	80%(2x3)		21 reps
	2.- P C +3P Jerks	65%(3x1-2)	70%(3x1-1)	75%(3x1-2)	80%(3x1-2)			21 reps
	3.- Back Squats	60%(3x5)	65%(2x5)	70%x4	75%x3	80%x3	83%x3	38 reps
	4.- Snatch Pull	85%(2x3)	90%(2x3)					12 reps
	5.- Ab work							
Day 2	1.- P Snatch bel kn	60%(2x3)	65%x3	70%x3	75%x3	80%(2x3)		21 reps
	2.- Jerk Behind N	65%x4	70%x4	75%x4	80%(3x3)			21 reps
	3.- Back Squats	60%x5	65%(2x5)	70%x3	75%x3	80%(2x3)	85%(2x3)	33 reps
	4.- SnatchPull	85%(2x3)	90%(2x3)					12 reps
	5.- Ab work							
Day 3	1.- Snatch	65%x3	70%x3	75%x3	80%x3	85%x3	90%x2	17 reps
	2.- C & J	65%x3	70%x3	75%x3	80%x3	85%x3	90%(2x2)	19 reps
	3.- Front Squat	70%(2x4)	75%(2x4)	80%x4	85%(2x3)			26 reps
	4.- Ab work							
Day 4	1.- Power Snatch	60%(2x3)	65%x3	70%x3	75%x3	80%(2x3)		21 reps
	2.- P C +3P Jerks	65%(3x1-2)	70%(3x1-1)	75%(3x1-2)	80%(3x1-2)			21 reps
	3.- Back Squats	60%x5	65%(2x5)	70%x3	75%x3	80%(2x3)	85%(2x3)	33 reps
Day 5	1.- Snatch	60%x3	65%(2x3)	70%x3	75%(2x3)	80%x3		21 reps
	2.- C & J	60%x3	65%(2x3)	70%x3	75%(2x3)	80%x3		21 reps
	3.- Back Squats	60%(3x5)	65%(2x5)	70%x3	75%x3	80%x3	85%x2	36 reps
	4.- SnatchPull	85%(3x4)	90%(2x3)					18 reps
Day 6	1.- Snatch	60%x3	65%(2x3)	70%x3	75%x3	80%x3	87%x1	21 reps
		95%(2x1)						
	2.- C & J	60%x3	65%(2x3)	70%x3	75%x3	80%(2x3)	87%x1	24 reps
		95%(2x1)						
	3.- Back Squats	60%(3x5)	65%(2x5)	70%x3	75%x2	80%x2	85%x2	36 reps
		90%x1	95%(2x1)					
	4.- SnatchPull	85%(2x3)	90%(2x3)					12 reps
Obs	Microcycle of preparation. 506 reps,snatch 122, C&J 127, squats,203, pulls 54							

Week 6	Macrocycle I. Mesocycle II. Microcycle II							
Day 1	1.- Power Snatch	70%(2x3)	75%x3	80%x3	83%(2x3)			18 reps
	2.- P Clean +3 PJ	60%(3x1-1)	65%(3x1-1)	70%(3x1-1)	80%(3x1-1)			18 reps
	3.- Back Squat	60%x5	65%x5	70%x5	75%x3	80%x3	83%(3x2)	27 reps
	4.- Snatch pull	85%(2x3)	90%(2x3)					12 reps
Day 2	1.- P Snatch B Kn	70%(2x3)	75%x3	80%x3	83%(2x3)			18 reps
	2.- Jerk b neck	60%x4	65%x4	70%x4	75%x3	80%(2x3)		21 reps
	3.- Front squat	70%(2x5)	75%(2x5)	80%x4	85%x3	87%x3		30 reps
	4.- Snatch pull	85%(2x3)	90%(2x3)					12 reps
Day 3	1.- Snatch	70%(2x3)	75%x3	80%x3	83%x3			15 reps
	2.- C & J	70%(2x3)	75%x3	80%x3	83%x3			15 reps
	3.- Back Squat	60%x5	65%x5	70%x5	75%(2x3)	80%(2x3)		27 reps
	4.- Snatch pull	85%(2x3)	90%(2x3)					12 reps
Day 4	1.- Power Snatch	70%(2x3)	75%x3	80%x3	83%x3			15 reps
	2.- 1 PC + 3 PJ	60%(3x1-2)	65%(3x1-1)	70%(3x1-1)				15 reps
	3.- Front squat	65%x5	70%x5	75%x5	80%(2x5)			25 reps
Day 5	1.- Snatch	60%x3	65%(2x3)	70%x3	75%x3	80%x3	85%x2	20 reps
	2.- C & J	60%x3	65%(2x3)	70%x3	75%x3	80%x3		20 reps
		85%x2						
	3.- Back Squat	70%(2x5)	75%(2x5)	80%x5	85%x3	90%x3		30 reps
	4.- Snatch pull	85%(2x3)	90%(2x3)					12 reps
Day 6	1.- Snatch	65%x3	70%(2x3)	75%x3	80%x3	85%x2		21 reps
		90%x2	95%(2x1)					
	2.- C & J	65%x3	70%(2x3)	75%x3	80%x2	85%x2	90%x2	23 reps
		95%x1	97%x1					
	3.- Back Squat	50%x4	55%x4	60%x4	65%x4	70%x3	75%x3	
		80%x3	85%x2	90%x1	95%x1	95%x1	100%x1	30 reps
	4.- Snatch pull	85%(2x3)	90%(2x3)					12 reps
Obs	Micrcycle of prep. 436 reps. Snatch 107, C&J 112, squats 169, pulls 48							

Week 7	Macrocycle I, Mesocycle II, Microcycle III						
Day 1	1.-Hang Snatch	60%(2x3)	65%x3	70%x3	75%(3x3)			21 reps
	2.- p Cl + 3 PJ	55%(3x1-1)	60%(3x1-1)	65%(3x1-1)	70%(3x1-1)	75%(3x1-1)	80%(3x1-1)	19 reps
		85%(3x1-2)						
	3.- Back squat	60%x5	65%x5	70%x5	75%x4	80%x4	83%(2x3)	29 reps
	4.- Santch Pulls	90%(2x3)	95%(2x3)					12 reps
Day 2	1.- Snatch	65%(2x3)	70%x3	75%x3	87%x3	85%(2x3)		21 reps
	2.- C&J	65%(2x3)	70%x3	75%x3	87%x3	85%(2x3)		21 reps
	3.- Front Squat	70%x5	75%x5	80%x4	85%x2	87%x2	90%x2	22 reps
		95%x2						
	4.- Santch Pulls	90%(2x3)	95%(2x3)					12 reps
Day 3	1.- Snatch	70%2x3	75%x3	80%x3	83%x3			15 reps
	2.- C&J	70%2x3	75%x3	80%x3	83%x3			15 reps
	3.- Back squat	60%x5	65%(2x5)	70%x3	75%x3	80%(2x3)		27 reps
Day 4	1.- P. Snatch	70%2x3	75%x3	80%x3	83%x3			15 reps
	2.- Jerk bn	70%2x3	75%(2x3)	80%x3	83%x3			18 reps
	3.- Front Squat	65%x5	70%x5	75%x4	80%(2x3)	85%(2x2)		24 reps
	4.- Snatch Bar	3X5						
	5.- C&J Bar	3X5						
Day 5	1.- Snatch	65%(2x3)	70%x3	75%x3	87%x3	85%x2		17 reps
	2.- C&J	65%(2x3)	70%x3	75%x3	87%x3	83%x2		17 reps
	3.- Back squat	60%x3	65%x3	70%x3	75%x3	80%(2x3)		
Day 6	1.- Snatch	65%x3	70%x3	75%x3	87%x3	85%x2	90%1	17 reps
		95%x1	100%x1					
	2.- C&J	65%x3	70%x3	75%x3	87%x3	85%x2	90%1	17 reps
		95%x1	100%x1					
Obs	Unloading	360 reps, snatch 103, C&J 107, squats120, pulls 30						

Week 8	Macrocycle I, Mesocycle II, Microcycle IV							
Day 1	1.-Power Snatch	70%(2x3)	75%x3	80%x3	83%(3x3)			21 reps
	2.-P Clean+3PJ	60%(3x1-1)	65%(3x1-2)	70%(3x1-1)	75%(3x1-1)	80%(3x1-2)		21 reps
	3.-Back Squat	60%x5	65%x5	70%x5	75%x3	80%x3	85%x3	87%(2x3)	30 reps
	4.- Snatch pull	90%(2x3)	95%(3x3)					12 reps
Day 2	1.- Snatch	70%(2x3)	75%x3	80%x3	83%x3	85%(2x3)		21 reps
	2.- C&J	75%(2x3)	70%(2x3)	80%x3	80%x3	85%x3	87%x3	21 reps
	3.- Front Squat	70%x5	75%(2x5)	80%x4	85%(2x3)	87%x3	90%x2	30 reps
	4.- Snatch pull	90%(2x3)	95%(2x3)					12 reps
Day 3	1.- Hang P. Snatch	65%(2x3)	70%x3	75%x3	80%(2x3)			15 reps
	2.- J behind neck	70%x3	75%x3	80%x3	85%x3	87%x3		15 reps
	3.- Back Squat	60%x5	65%x5	70%x3	75%x3	80%(2x3)		22 reps
Day 4	1.-P Snatch	70%(2x3)	75%x3	80%(2x3)	83% x3			18 reps
	2.-P Clean+3PJ	60%(3x1-1)	65%(3x1-1)	70%(3x1-1)	75%(3x1-1)	80%(3x1-1)	85%(3x1-2)	21 reps
	3.- Front Squat	65%x5	70%x5	75%x5	80%(2x5)			25 reps
Day 5	1.- Snatch	70%(2x3)	75%x3	80%x3	83%x3	85%(2x3)		21 reps
	2.- C & J	75%(2x3)	70%(2x3)	80%x3	80%x3	85%x3	87%x3	21 reps
	3.- Back Squat	60%x5	65%x5	70%x5	75%x4	80%x3	85%x3	87%(2x3)	31 reps
	4.- Snatch pull	90%(2x3)	95%(2x3)					12 reps
Day 6	1.- Snatch	65%x3	70%(2x3)	75%x3	80%x3	85%x2	90%x2	95%x1	20 reps
	2.- C & J	50%x3	55%(2x3)	60%x3	65%x3	70%x2	75%x2	80%x2	24 reps
		85%x1	90%x1	95%x1	100%x1			
	3.- Back Squat	50%x4	55%x4	60%x4	65%x4	70%x3	75%x3	80%x3	
		85%x2	90%x2	95%x1	100%x1			
	4.- Snatch pull	90%(2x3)	95%(2x3)					12 reps
Obs	Microcycle of preparation. 459 reps. Snatch 116 reps. C & J 123 reps. Squats 169 reps. Pulls 51 reps							

Week 9	Macrocycle I, Mesocycle III, Microcycle I						
Day 1	1.- Snatch	70%(2x3)	75%x3	80%x3	83%(3x3)			21 reps
	2.- C & J	70%(2x3)	75%x3	80%x3	83%(3x3)			21 reps
	3.- Back squat	60%x5	65%x5	70%x5	75%3	80%x3	83%(2x3)	27 reps
	4.- Ab work							
Day 2	1.- Snatch	65%(2x3)	70%(2x3)	75%(3x3)				21 reps
	2.- C & J	65%(2x3)	70%(2x3)	75%(3x3)				21 reps
	3.- Front squat	60%x5	65%x5	70%x5	75%(2x3)	80%x3	83%(2x3)	30 reps
	4.- Ab work							
Day 3	1.- Hang Snatch	65%(2x3)	70%x3	75%(3x3)				18 reps
	2.- Jerk b neck	65%(2x3)	70%x3	75%(2x3)				15 reps
	3.- Back squat	60%x5	65%x5	70%x4	75%3	80%(2x3)		23 reps
Day 4	1.- Snatch	65%x3	70%x(2x3)	75%(2x3)				15 reps
	2.- C&J	65%x3	70%x(2x3)	75%(2x3)				15 reps
		65%x5	70%x5	75%x5	80%(2x3)			21 reps
Day 5	1.- Snatch	65%x3	70%x3	75%x2	80%x2	85%x2	90%x2	Max out
		95%x1	100%x1	105%x1				day
	2.- C&J	65%x3	70%x3	75%x2	80%x2	85%x2	90%x2	
		95%x1	100%x1	105%x1				
Day 6	Sauna, light jogg 10 minutes, body building exercises with light weights, stretching out.							
Obs	Microcycle of unloading. Reps 248. Snatch 75, C&J 72, squats 102							

Week 10	Macrocycle I. Mesocycle III. Microcycle II							
Day 1	1.- Power Snatch	60%(2x4)	65%(3x3)	70%x3	75%(2x3)			26 reps
	2.- P Cl + 3 P J	65%(3x1-1)2	70%(3x1-1)2	75%(3x1-1)3	80%(3x1-)2			27 reps
	3.- Back Squats	60%(2x5)	65%(2x5)	70%(2x5)	75%(2x3)	80%x3	83%(2x3)	45 reps
	4.- Snatch Pull	90%(2x3)	93%(2x3)					12 reps
Day 2	1.- P Snatch b knee	60%(2x4)	65%(2x3)	70%x3	75%(2x3)			26 reps
	2.- Jerk behind neck	65%(2x3)	70%(2x3)	75%(2x3)	80%(2x3)			24 reps
	3.- Back Squats	60%(2x5)	65%(2x5)	70%(2x5)	75%4	80%x3	83%(2x3)	43 reps
	4.- Snatch Pull	90%(2x3)	93%(2x3)					12 reps
Day 3	1.- Power Snatch	60%x3	65%(2x3)	70%x3	75%(2x3)			18 reps
	2.- Jerk behind neck	60%x5	70%x5	70%(2x3)	75%(2x3)			20 reps
	3.- Front squats	70%(2x5)	75%(2x5)	80%(2x4)	85%(2x4)			43 reps
Day 4	1.- Power Snatch	60%x4	65%x3	70%(2x3)	75%(2x3)	80%x3		22 reps
	2.- PC + 4PJ	60%(4x1-1)2	65%(4x1-1)2	70%(4x1-1)2				24 reps
	3.- Front squats	65%x5	70%(2x5)	75%(2x4)	80%x4	85%x3	90%(2x3)	12 reps
Day 5	1.- Snatch	60%x3	65%(2x3)	70%x3	75%x3	80%(3x3)		24 reps
	2.- C&J	60%(2x3)	65%(2x3)	70%x3	75%x3	80%(3x3)		27 reps
	3.- Back Squats	50%(2x5)	55%x5	60%x5	65%4	70%4	75%x3	41 reps
		80%x3	85%x3	90%(2x2)				
	4.- Snatch Pull	90%(2x3)	93%(2x3)					12 reps
Day 6	1.- Snatch	60%x3	65%(2x3)	70%x3	75%x3	80%x3	85%x2	25 reps
		87%x1	70%x2	90%(2x1)				
	2.- C&J	60%x3	65%(2x3)	70%x3	75%x3	80%x3	85%x3	25 reps
		87%x2	70%x2	90%(2x1)				
	3.- Back Squats	87%x1	70%x2	90%(2x1)				32 reps
		80%x3	85%x3	90%(2x2)	95%x1	100%x1		
	4.- Snatch Pull	90%(3x3)	93%(2x3)					15 reps
Obs	High in Volume. 594 reps, 138 snatch, 149 C&J, 244 squats, 63 pulls							

Week 11	Macrocycle I. Mesocycle III. Microcycle III								
Day 1	1.- Power Snatch	60%x4	65%(2x3)	70%x3	75%x3	80%x3	83%(2x2)			23 reps
	2.- PCl+3 PJ	65%(3x1-1)	70%(3x1-1)3	75%(3x1-1)	78%(3x1-1)2					24 reps
	3.- Back squat	55%x5	60%x5	65%(2x5)	70%(2x3)	75%x3	80%x3	85%x3		35 reps
	4.- Snatch Pulls	90%(2x3)	93%(2x3)							12 reps
Day 2	1.- P Snatch b knee	60%x4	65%x3	70%(2x3)	75%x3	80%x3				19 reps
	2.- Back squat + Jerk	45%(2x3)	50%(2x3)	55%(2x3)	60%(2x3)					24 reps
	3.- Back squats	60%x5	65%x5	70%(2x3)	75%x3	80%x3	85%(2x3)			28 reps
	4.- Snatch Pulls	90%(2x3)	93%(2x3)							12 reps
Day 3	1.- Power Snatch	60%x3	65%(2x3)	70%x3	75%(2x3)					18 reps
	2.- Jerk behind neck	65%x5	70%x5	75%(2x3)	78%(2x3)					20 reps
	3.- Front squat	70%x5	75%(2x5)	80%(2x4)	85%x4	90%x2				29 reps
Day 4	1.- Power Snatch	60%x4	65%(2x3)	70%x3	75%x3	80%x3	83%(2x2)			23 reps
	2.- P Cl + fro squ+PJ	60%(4x1-1)2	65%(4x1-1)2	70%94x1-1)2						24 reps
	3.-Front squat	70%x5	75%(2x4)	80%x4	85%x3	90%(2x3)				26 reps
Day 5	1.- Snatch	65%x3	70%x3	75%(2x3)	80%x3	85%x3	87%(2x2)			22 reps
	2.- C & J	60%x3	65%x3	70%(2x3)	75%(2x3)	80%x3	85%(2x2)			25 reps
	3.- Back Squats	50%x5	55%x5	60%x5	65%x3	70%x3	75%x3	80%x3	85%x3	34 reps
		88%(2x2)								
	4.- Snatch Pulls	90%(2x3)	93%(2x3)							12 reps
Day 6	1.- Snatch	55%x3	60%x3	65%x3	70%x3	75%x3	80%x2	85%x1	65%x2	22 reps
		92%(2x1)								
	2.- C & J	50%x3	55%(2x3)	60%x3	65%x3	70%x3	75%x2	80%x1	85%x1	24 reps
		90%(2x1)								
	3.- Back squats	45%x5	50%x5	55%x5	60%x4	65%x3	70%x3	75%x3	80%x3	35 reps
		85%x2	90%x2	93%x1	96%x1					
	4.- Snatch Pulls	90%(2x3)	93%(2x3)							12 reps
Obs	High volume. 518 reps. 127 Snatch. 141 C&J. 187 squats. 63 pulls								

Week 12	Macrocycle I. Mesocycle III. Microcycle IV - Competition modeling or control test							
Day 1	1.- Snatch	65%(2x3)	70%x3	75%x3	80%(3x3)			21 reps
	2.- C&J	65%(2x3)	70%x3	75%x3	80%(3x3)			21 reps
	3.- Back Squat	55%x5	60%x5	65%x4	70%x3	75%x3	80%x3	29 reps
		85%x3						
	4.- Snatch pull	90%(2x3)	93%(2x3)					12 reps
Day 2	1.- Snatch	65%(2x3)	70%(2x3)	75%(3x3)				21 reps
	2.- C&J	65%(2x3)	70%(2x3)	75%(3x3)				21 reps
	3.- Front Squat	70%x5	75%(2x5)	80%x4	85%(2x3)	87%x3	90%(2x1)	30 reps
Day 3	1.- Hang Snatch	65%x3	70%x3	75%x3	80%(3x3)			18 reps
	2.- Jerk B neck	65%x3	65%x3	70%x3	75%(2x3)			15 reps
	3.- Back Squat	55%x5	60%x5	65%x4	70%x3	75%x3	80%x3	23 reps
Day 4	1.- Snatch	65%(2x3)	70%x3	75%x3	80%(2x3)			18 reps
	2.- C&J	60%(2x3)	65%x3	70%x3	75%x3	77%(2x3)		21 reps
	3.- Back Squat	55%x5	60%x5	65%x4	70%x3	75%x3	80%x3	29 reps
		85%(2x3)						
Day 5	1.- Snatch	65%x3	70%(2x3)	75%(2x3)				15 reps
	2.- C&J	60%(2x3)	65%(2x3)	70%x3				15 reps
	3.- Front Squat	65%x5	70%x5	75%x5	80%(2x3)			21 reps
Day 6	1.- Snatch	65%x3	70%(2x3)	75%x3	80%x2	85%x1	90%x1	21 reps
		95%x1	70%x2	100%x1	105%x1			
	2.- C&J	65%x3	70%(2x3)	75%x3	80%x2	85%x1	90%x1	21 reps
		95%x1	70%x2	100%x1	105%x1			
Obs	Microcycle of unloading. 338 reps. Snatch 93. C&J 92. Squats 129. Pulls 24. Test control							

Gwendolyn Sisto and Ivan Rojas

Works Cited

Anne Houtman, M. S.-C. (2016, January 7). *Testing the Iceman*, Chapter 22. In M. S.-C. Anne Houtman, *Biology Now* (pp. 388-405). not provided: W W Norton & Company Incorporated. Retrieved January 7, 2016, from Wim Hof Method: http://www.wimhofmethod.com/uploads/kcfinder/files/biology-now-chapter-22-Wim-Hof.pdf

Europe, N. i. (2011-2016). A survey of optimal height by weight class as reported by coaches of elite lifters. (I. Rojas, Interviewer)

Hererra, Dr. A. (2012). Risto Sports Soviet System Certification. Risto Sports.

Herrera, Dr. A. (2012). (G. S. Ivan Rojas, Interviewer)

Hof, I. (2015, June). *Innerfire*. Retrieved from www.innerfire.nl: www.wimhofmethod.com

Ivan Rojas, G. S. (2015). *Kazakhstan Weightlifting System for Elite Athletes*. BookCrafters, Parker, Colorado

Jam, D. B. (2014). *Paradigm Shifts: Use of Ice & NSAIDs Post Acute Soft Tissue Injuries*. http://physicaltherapyweb.com/paradigm-shifts-use-ice-nsaids-post-acute-soft-tissue-injuries-part-1-2/.

Medvedev, A. (1985). *System of multi-year training for Weightlifting*. Moscow.

Nat Arem, D. B. (Director). (2016). DIMAS - Part Two - *"The Right System at the Right Time"* [Motion Picture].

Nunez, D. (2014, July). *Ice therapy and effect on training with coahc and Olympic Gold Medalist Daniel Nunez*. (I. Rojas, Interviewer)

Paakkonen, T., & Leppaluoto, J. (2002). *Cold Exposure and Hormonal Secretion: A Review*. International Journal Circumpolar Health, 61, 265-276.

Perez, C. (Unknown). *Introduction to technique*. Cuba: UCCFD Manuel Fajardo.

Philosophical realism. (2016, 12 25). Retrieved from Wikipedia: https://en.wikipedia.org/wiki/Philosophical_realism

Rojas, I. (2014, May). *Observations of Cuban training, while training in Cuba 1988 and 1999.* (G. Sisto, Interviewer)

Rosenthal, I. (1964). *Dictionary of Marxist Philosophy.* Moscow.

Sport.Ru.Ru. R I of N, http://sport.rin.ru/cgi-bin/index1.pl?a=vid_sporta_izv_persona&vid sporta =10&persona_id=3118. Accessed 25 Nov. 2016.

Medvedev, Alexi. *Three Periods of the Snatch and Clean Jerk.* December 1988 - Volume 10 - Issue 6 - ppg 33-38

List of citations by Dr. Herrera from 2012 Soviet System Certification:

Медведев АС, Масалъгин Н.А, Фролов В.И., Эррера А.Г.О взаимосвязи параметров толчка штанги от груди // Теория и практика физической культуры. 1981. № 6. С. 6—7.

-Медведев АС, Масалъгин Н.А, Эррера АГ., Фролов В.И.Классификация толчковых упражнений в подъеме штанги от груди и методика их применения в зависимости от квалификации тяжелоатлетов // Тяжелая атлетика. М.: Физкультура и спорт,1982

-Медведев А.С., Масальгин Н.А., Эррера А.Г.К., Лукашев А.А., Верхошанский Ю.В., Новиков П.С. Взаимосвязь технической и специальной физической подготовленности у тяжелоатлетов высокой квалификации в толчке штанги от груди. Методическое пособие. РИО ГЦОЛИФК, М., 1991 г.

Эррера Корзо Гильермо Альфредо. Методика совершенствования техники толчка штанги от груди в процессе становления спортивного мастерства : Автореф. дис. канд. пед. наук. М., 1981

-Эррера А.Г.К. Методика совершенствования техники толчка штанги от груди в процессе становления спортивного мастерства: Автореф. канд. дис. - М.: тип. МЭИ, 1995.

About the Authors

Gwendolyn Sisto

Gwendolyn Sisto is many things. Academically, she is Rocket Scientist, who holds a Masters of Science from MIT in Aeronautics and Astronautics and a Bachelors of Science from Georgia Tech. She has worked for many years in the Aerospace industry and has been featured in Georgia Tech's "30 under 30" and MIT alumni association's "I look like an engineer" campaign.

She is also a highly decorated weightlifter and has helped advance the sport over the last two decades. She won or medaled far over 25 times in National USA Weightlifting Competitions. She has competed internationally for Team USA at least four times, and competed at an Olympic Trial. She helped expose weightlifting to the broader fitness world. She was the Meet Director of the first ever weightlifting competition at the Mr. Olympia Expo, arguably the most important fitness expo in the world. Gwen also co-founded Risto Sports, which has sponsored USAW, including the 2012 Olympic Team podium attire, and numerous athletes over the years. She has studied weightlifting programming from around the world the last 14 years alongside Coach Ivan Rojas and other experts.

Photo 4 - Author Gwendolyn Sisto Snatching 92kg at the 2014 Risto Olympia Cup presented by AlaskaFit Productions at the Mr Olympia weekend. Photo by Gwendolyn Rojas.

Ivan Rojas

Ivan Rojas is an international man of weightlifting. He has been in the sport well over 30 years. As an athlete, he competed at the highest levels and has also coached at the highest levels. He was most recently the coach of the Panama National Team. He was a National Coach of the 2010 USA World University Team which won 15 medals. He also was a coach of the US National 13 and under team in 2014.

Ivan was privileged to formally study weightlifting during the 1980's in Soviet and Eastern-bloc countries. Ivan formally studied the Soviet weightlifting system in Poland, Cuba, the former Soviet Union (now Russia), and East Germany. Along with Gwen, he has continued to study the evolution of the system in Kazakhstan, China, Bulgaria, Romania, and Colombia.

Photo 5 - Coach Ivan Rojas studying the Kazakh system in Astana, Kazakhstan. Photo by Gwendolyn Rojas.

Athletes with whom Ivan has worked include:

Athlete	Country	Comments
Maryam Usman	Nigeria	Trained at Risto Sports multiple months in 2013. Won 2014 Commonwealth Games. She is also a 2008 Olympic Bronze Medalist and a World Medalist.
Luz Mercedes Acosta	Mexico	Trained at Risto Sports prior to the 2011 Pan Am Games. She won the bronze medal at the 2012 Olympic Games.
Diego Salazar	Colombia	Diego trained at Risto Sports multiple times. He is an Olympic Silver Medalist
Carlos Andica	Colombia	Trained multiple times at Risto Sports. Broke Pan Am Games clean and jerk record after work with Risto Sports, multiple times international medalist.
Annie Thorisdottir	Iceland	Two time CrossFit Games Champion
Johnny Andica	Colombia	Pan Am Champion, multiple time international medalist
Gwendolyn Sisto	USA	Competed at US Olympic Trials, 5th World University Championships, 8+ National Teams. Various national titles.
Gwendolyn Rojas	USA	National 13 & under team, won 13 & under international invitational, invited to compete at Kazakhstan Youth nationals, multiple time USA Youth National Champion
Venessa Quinones	Colombia	Qualified for the Pan Am team after training at Risto Sports. Pan Am medalist.
Rocio Navarro	Panama	Panama National Team, highest ranked female lifter in Central America
Ariel Batista	Panama	Panama National Team, international competitor
Lesbia Cruz	Guatemala	Guatemalan National Team, international competitor
Javier Castillo	Guatemala	Guatemalan National Team
Elio Guerra	Cuba	Pan am champion
Neisi Dajomes	Ecuador	Multiple time Junior World Champion, Youth World Champion. 2016 Olympian.
Jessica Weisman	USA	2015 World Masters Champion, 2016 World Masters Silver Medalist

Photo 6 - Ivan and Gwen embracing after Gwen broke the 200kg mark at the 2014 Risto Olympia Cup. Photo by Gwendolyn Rojas.

About Risto Sports

Risto Sports was founded by Coach Ivan Rojas and Gwendolyn Sisto, an MIT rocket scientist who has competed numerous times for Team USA. Ivan, through Olympic solidarity, trained and studied weightlifting around the world. This included training behind the iron curtain in former Eastern Block countries such as the USSR, East Germany, Cuba, and Bulgaria.

Since then, Gwen and Ivan have worked with some of the best coaches in the world, including the coaches of Kazakhstan, to bring you the absolute best weightlifting products – that means training programs, shoes, wrist wraps, knee wraps, books, singlets, compression pants and DVD's – to you.

Photo 7 - Full Grain Leather weightlifting shoe by Risto Sports. Photo by Gwendolyn Sisto.

On top of this, **Risto Sports** believes that – Yes, you can have high performance products that are: affordable, high performance, fair trade made, made of quality materials such as leather, that look good, use many locally sourced materials, and are Made in the USA or the Americas.

Photo 8- Russian Style weightlifting boots by Risto Sports, with solid wood heel and top grain leather. Perfect for Soviet training! Photo by Gwendolyn Sisto.

Photo 9 - Olympic silver medallist Diego Salazar with Coach Ivan Rojas at Risto Sports. Photo by Gwendolyn Sisto.

Why we care about bringing you the best products and services

Risto Sports was started by a dream. When Ivan was a lifter, he dreamt that he was in the office of the Bulgaria Weightlifting Federation, and that he was surrounded by weightlifting shoes on display. Years later, when training for the 2008 Olympic Trials, Ivan and Gwen went to Bulgaria and were invited to the office of the Bulgarian Federation General Secretary. Like Ivan's dream, he was surrounded by displays; though, instead of shoes, they were covered in trophies from world cups and championships that the Bulgarian national Team had won. Shortly after, Ivan and Gwen had met Stefan Botev who sold them the first shipment of leather weightlifting shoes that Gwen and Ivan would bring to the USA for the benefit all strength athletes. Whereas, at the time, there was only one brand of weightlifting shoe even available in the USA, which were of declining design and quality.

Since then, Ivan and Gwen created Risto Sports for the purpose of supporting and promoting Olympic weightlifting and related strength sports. Risto Sports, particularly, serves the underserved strength sport market including: weightlifting, CrossFit, bodybuilding, powerlifting, and strongman.

What makes Risto Sports unique from other brands is that all of Risto Sports products are actually designed by weightlifting experts. In effect, our customers will get the most out of their lifting experience by using our products.

Lightning Source UK Ltd.
Milton Keynes UK
UKHW020843140720
366502UK00003B/40